SCALING FOR SUCCESS

SCALING

FOR

SUCCESS

People Priorities
for High-Growth
Organizations

ANDREW BARTLOW
and T. BRAD HARRIS

Columbia Business School
Publishing

Columbia University Press
Publishers Since 1893
New York   Chichester, West Sussex
cup.columbia.edu
Copyright © 2021 Andrew Bartlow and T. Brad Harris

Library of Congress Cataloging-in-Publication Data
Names: Bartlow, Andrew, author. | Harris, T. Brad, author.
Title: Scaling for success : people priorities for high-growth organizations /
Andrew Bartlow and T. Brad Harris.
Description: 1 Edition. | New York City : Columbia University Press, 2021. |
Includes bibliographical references and index.
Identifiers: LCCN 2020044081 (print) | LCCN 2020044082 (ebook) |
ISBN 9780231194440 (hardback) | ISBN 9780231550833 (ebook)
Subjects: LCSH: New business enterprises—Management. | Personnel management.
| Employees—Recruiting. | Employee selection. | Business planning.
Classification: LCC HD62.5 .B377 2021 (print) | LCC HD62.5 (ebook) |
DDC 658.3/01—dc23
LC record available at https://lccn.loc.gov/2020044081
LC ebook record available at https://lccn.loc.gov/2020044082

Cover design: Noah Arlow

For the dreamers and for the doers. We hope to lighten your load just a little.

—AB

For all the builders trying to make something better, bigger.

—BH

CONTENTS

ACKNOWLEDGMENTS

We owe a debt of gratitude to the many individuals who helped us bring this book to fruition. Although it is impossible to mention everyone who has provided some measure of support along the way, we do want to acknowledge those who have been especially instrumental in this process.

First, to the friends and professional colleagues who gave their time to be interviewed during our research for the book, offered a quote or provided a friendly review, wrote a chapter introduction, or just provided a much needed and well-timed word of encouragement: Cara Allamano, David Allen, Guissu Raafat Baier, Luke Beseda, Wendy Boswell, Nichelle Carpenter, Michael Case, Peter Clarke, Steve Conaton, Patrick Downes, Gentzy Franz, Jesse Freese, Richard Gardner, Quasar Hamirani, David Hanrahan, Saydeah Howard, Laura Huang, Kaifeng Jiang, Brad Kirkman, Amit Kramer, Carmela Krantz, Ning Li, Steve McElfresh, Blair Middlebrook, Ashish Raina, Sara Roberts, Kati Ryan, Michael Sherrod, Eric Steinert, Brian Swider, and Melissa Taunton.

Second, to the kind and very patient folks who helped us navigate the publication process, including our editors at Columbia University Press, Brian Smith and Myles Thompson, for giving us a shot; our former editor and now extremely gracious friend Margo Beth Fleming, for offering so much useful advice; and the super talented group, Amy Anderson,

Lauren Miller, Cole Noone, and Ryan Winn, who helped us sort out so many little things along the way.

Third, to our employers and other affiliated organizations that provided us a notable measure of opportunity to sit down and write a book, including Series B Consulting, The Neeley School of Business at Texas Christian University, and the School of Labor and Employment Relations at the University of Illinois at Urbana-Champaign. In this same spirit, we also want to thank the Texas Christian University MBA students who took our "Scaling for Success" class. They not only pushed us to think more critically about our ideas for this book but also confirmed that there are many incredibly bright minds out there with ideas worth scaling.

Finally, to our families, for their immeasurable support and motivation along the way.

SCALING FOR SUCCESS

1

Scaling for Success

The purpose of this book is to help startup founders and executives pursuing rapid growth develop and execute an effective *people strategy* (i.e., recruiting, acquiring, and ultimately leveraging an organization's human capital for strategic success). If you are currently in the midst of accelerated growth, or even *hyper*growth (>50 percent headcount growth per year), you undoubtedly know what an exciting and terrifying process it can be. In many cases, rapid headcount growth follows a funding event, which provides fuel that can either burn up the competition or burn down the house from the inside. Our goal is to help your company successfully scale up.

Leading a high-growth startup is unlike many other challenges, both professionally and personally. You and your company have probably survived early challenges thanks to your ability to adapt to the needs of the market. As your company grows, however, it will inevitably hit a breaking point—and several more breaking points if you are doing things right. Borrowing from bestselling author and executive coach Marshall Goldsmith, you must realize that *what got you here won't get you there.*[1] Things will start falling apart faster than they can be fixed. Hard work, quick thinking, and great relationships become mere prerequisites. Hiring smart people and turning them loose will not cut it anymore. You need to quickly learn how to effectively plan, delegate, and communicate. You need new systems and processes that align an ever-growing number of employees with the right priorities. *You need a plan.*

Recent empirical research indicates that management practices are a more potent differentiator of top versus bottom organizational performers than other popular factors such as great tech, R&D expenditures, and even worker skills.[2] This conclusion echoes myriad scholarly and practical opinions on the critical role of people management.[3] Melissa Taunton, partner with New Enterprise Associates (a top-tier venture capital firm with approximately $20 billion under management), says, "People management is the artery of your organization. You can have a great idea, but you can't execute it without a great team." Similarly, another highly experienced talent partner at a top-tier venture capital (VC) firm shared this: "Thinking about how to recruit and build a strong organization is very different than what most founders have spent most of their time on prior to a major funding round. Founders are afraid they will get it wrong and [benefit from getting] experienced help. While it is difficult to measure the impact of people and management practices, we have seen companies struggle time and again with the same issues. We have seen just about everything."[4] Finally, business school professors Ranjay Gulati (Harvard) and Alicia DeSantola (Washington) write, "As just about any rapidly growing startup will attest, scaling up is challenging. Market crashes, unreliable supply and distribution partners, fierce rivals, and plenty of other external forces can buffet firms. But that doesn't mean companies need to be chaotic on the inside. Effective internal organization frees them up to keep pursuing new opportunities and brings long-term survival within reach."[5]

The following scenario describes a pattern among high-growth startups:

> A promising company has recently raised a new round of venture capital and is now trying to nearly double its staff in the next year. The founding team has been reliant on their personal networks and search firms to find talent so far, but they know that approach will not scale. They need to determine what new roles need to be filled, in what sequence, with defined skills, capabilities, and responsibilities—and how to attract and select those candidates in a highly competitive talent market.
>
> When the team finds an interested candidate that they want to hire, they must present a package of pay, equity, perks, and programs that will convince the target to join the company. The new hire needs to be effectively provisioned, informed of how to get things done within the organization, and understand what things are most urgent

and important. In a chaotic startup environment, role and goal clarity are often fuzzy, in part due to inadequate planning, rapidly changing priorities, and inconsistent messages from leadership.

Early employees are hesitant about changes to people and management practices, and even worry that the company's cultural "soul" is in danger.[6] To relieve these fears, the leadership team spends countless hours trying to articulate and communicate a vision, mission, and core values for the organization—which are usually so watered down in an attempt to appeal to everyone that they are useless. Costly incentive plans and administratively intensive performance management processes are implemented to motivate and align employees to the most important priorities, but those priorities are usually unclear, unstable, and often conflicting.

Employee engagement survey scores decrease and turnover increases. Replacing employees becomes more difficult as the remaining managers are stretched to the breaking point. Perks and programs are introduced to improve morale, and some senior leaders are changed out. Alas, these tactics only add to the pressure and sense of chaos as more disruption is introduced and core issues are not adequately addressed. Employees become more frustrated and less committed. Product road maps fall behind schedule. Operating results do not meet expectations. The pressure and anxiety snowballs, and the future of a once-promising startup begins to look bleak.

If you have been around even a few startups, you have probably seen or heard similar stories.

As a company grows, its processes and practices must evolve to support that growth. Key people practices that need to be addressed during a company's evolution include workforce planning, new hire sourcing, selection and onboarding processes, compensation and benefits programs, training and development, company culture and communications, goal setting and performance management practices, a company's approach to legal and compliance issues, plus resourcing the HR/people function supporting all of these activities. Every situation is different, but the good news is that meaningful similarities, and thus lessons, usually hold across all sorts of organizations.[7] To that end, this book is designed to help you think proactively about the most critical people management challenges you will face during rapid growth and develop solutions that enable you to find success. Will it give you all the answers in a neat Cliff's Notes package that you can absorb in ninety seconds or less? Of course not. Although predictable, these issues are serious, and sufficient thought and context is required to successfully address them.

Who Should Read This Book?

This book is for leaders who want pragmatic, actionable advice for addressing common management issues that emerge during periods of rapid growth. Our writing is specifically targeted toward founders/CEOs and senior leaders of high-growth venture-backed startups with Series A, B, and perhaps C seed funding. Although this tightly defined audience is positioned to benefit most directly from this work, leaders outside of the startup and venture capital community can also learn valuable lessons. We feel our work adds to the body of knowledge available to investors, entrepreneurs, people managers at any organization, business school students, and all those who support the startup community. In subsequent chapters, we offer templates and frameworks that you can apply immediately. The lessons offered here are rooted in our consulting work, rigorous management research, personal experiences, and the experiences of many other talented contributors, including chief people officers (CPOs), venture capital talent partners (TPs), and some of the most elite and experienced service providers to the startup community.

Many books relate to and precede our work, and our favorites include Hoffman and Yeh's *Blitzscaling*, Gil's *High Growth Handbook*, Belsky's *The Messy Middle*, McGrath and MacMillan's *The Entrepreneurial Mindset*, Reis's *The Lean Startup*, Kawasaki's *Art of the Start*, and Blumberg's *Startup CEO*.[8] Although we share some necessary content overlap with these works, our book is unique in focusing exclusively on the people management practices needed to survive and thrive in a high-growth environment at an early startup stage. A caveat worth noting: Even though our book is about people management practices, i.e., human resources (HR) practices, don't let the HR label fool you. All managers, not just HR managers, are in the business of managing talent. In fact, many organizations we work with have tiny or nonexistent HR departments, which makes their people management capacities even more critical! Even in later-stage startups when formal HR professionals exist, high-growth phases introduce some unique challenges that are not well-addressed in more traditional texts. Developing a "people playbook" is a must for startup leaders serious about growing and surviving.

Who Should *Not* Read This Book?

This book is *not* for those looking for the next management fad or silver bullet pseudoscience. Nor is it for those who want to mirror the freewheeling and free spending management practices of a unicorn (i.e., private companies with a valuation >$1 billion). We are supportive of aspirational goals, but there is a fundamental difference between a "typical" high-growth startup and the unicorns we read about in popular media. Most high-growth companies are resource constrained and must be discerning in how they expend their limited financial and human resources.[9] Conversely, only a few (very well-known) companies have the almost limitless resources to invest excessively in the attraction, retention, and utilization of their talent. Unicorns can afford to make more mistakes than most startups—their killer product and tremendous market demand will carry them through many challenges.

Separately, experienced founders/CEOs and people leaders with experience across multiple startups may find some of our themes and key points familiar. However, doctors tend to make the worst patients. Experienced operators can be at great risk of copying and pasting so-called best practices from their prior organizations into their newest company—and those practices often do not make sense in their current context. If you are not willing to acknowledge the risks of a "lift and shift" approach, we can't help you. For all others, keep reading. You may be surprised how even minor tweaks to prior practices can make a big difference.

Are You Ready?

Before we dive in, we want to warn you: To survive and thrive in a high-growth startup, your organization's key leaders must be willing and ready to adapt their management practices to your company's ever-changing situation. This will not be easy, but if you are willing to put in the work and direct your efforts toward smart strategies, it can be one of the most rewarding experiences of your professional (and perhaps even personal) life.

We have had the privilege to observe and work alongside many founders and leaders of high-growth startups. Most of these people are extremely smart and capable individuals with good intentions, but these leaders are rarely fully prepared to adapt their deeply ingrained management style. They have been successful in building a company. They

Figure 1.1
Mule driver

attracted venture funding. They may have hundreds of employees and tens of millions of dollars in annual revenues. However, the behaviors that enabled them to become successful entrepreneurs are often at odds with the behaviors that will help their companies continue to grow. Consider the following lighthearted, but nevertheless common, archetypes: *mule drivers* and *prophets*.

A mule driver fills the wagon with as many items as possible, hitches up as many mules as needed to pull the wagon, and usually does not take particularly good care of those mules (figure 1.1). The mule driver shouts frequently to get those "lazy" mules to trudge faster toward an often-erroneous destination known only to the mule driver. The mule driver is not necessarily ill-intentioned, but the driver believes that the mules lack intelligence, are readily replaceable, and will be lost without constant "encouragement" (which may be a carrot but is just as frequently a stick).

In a startup context, mule drivers resist hiring functional leaders and skilled managers, trusting only themselves to steer their team. They also surround themselves with relatively inexperienced and lower-skilled employees who are expected only to promptly execute the directions of the mule driver. We saw this situation develop firsthand with a strong-minded and previously successful founder. "Diane" wanted to be involved in nearly every decision and struggled to delegate tasks. She did not trust her people.

Ironically, her predisposition for distrust was only aggravated by her decision to construct a junior staff of relatively low-skilled (and lower-paid) individuals in most roles. Her approach was considered wisely frugal when the company was small, but it became untenable (and almost an outright disaster) as the company began trying to scale. Indeed, the organization went through more than a year of constant churn and dissatisfaction due to her micromanagement. Thankfully, Diane eventually "saw the light" (thanks in part to executive coaching and several calls from VCs and board members) and figured out that she needed to invest in and empower her team's talent for her business to effectively scale.

Other founders assume the role of a prophet. The prophet is a master storyteller and is remarkably effective at convincing others to follow (figure 1.2). However, when the real work needs to be done, or difficult decisions need to be made, the prophet is hard to find. Prophets are far more comfortable studying in their ivory towers or speaking to adoring masses than they are doing the dirty work. Prophets surround themselves with highly skilled disciples who are committed to their cause, but they fail to provide those followers with meaningful direction. Prophets are averse to conflict, avoid difficult decisions, and often refuse to acknowledge bad

Figure 1.2
Prophet

news or problems; they see endless possibilities in an irrationally positive, borderline delusional future.

We once witnessed a leader surround himself with world-class talent genuinely committed to the mission of the organization. "Nadim's" charisma and vision attracted high-caliber employees and substantial outside investment to pursue his ideas. Unfortunately, Nadim and his team proved incapable of executing on those ideas. Although he was very comfortable delegating to others (unlike the mule driver), he struggled to hold people accountable, never defined clear roles or objectives, and failed to make difficult decisions when big ideas met resistance or finite resources needed to be thoughtfully allocated. Sadly, his organization was shuttered after burning through hundreds of millions of dollars.

We suspect these archetypes are familiar to some of you. Maybe you have worked closely with someone who has these tendencies, or perhaps you yourself exhibit some of them. Whatever the case, we hope the conclusion is obvious: Neither the mule driver's nor the prophet's entrepreneurial style is ideal or sustainable as an organization grows and matures. A formerly successful captain of a single pirate ship must adapt her style to become more like an admiral in the Navy.[10] The natural curiosity and entrepreneurial spirit your organization and its leaders proudly proclaimed will feel at odds with the need to establish and maintain the basic systems and structure required by a complex organization. Survival requires a thoughtful and sometimes painfully self-aware consideration of how effectively *you* are operating within your rapidly evolving organization. To this end, we echo the encouraging words of leadership authors Linda Hill (professor at Harvard Business School) and Kent Lineback (former business executive): "If you still need to make progress on your journey, that should spur you to action, not discourage you. You can become what you want and need to be."[11]

What Are the Core Lessons of This Book?

Throughout the book we offer a variety of tips, traps, and practical tools for startup leaders. However, a few overarching themes span across chapters and concepts:

1. **Have a plan.** It is critical to develop and maintain an evolving people management strategy as your organization grows and changes. In the chaos of startup life, this simple step is surprisingly easy to miss.

2. **Master (only) the basics.** A finite number of core activities will create the foundation for further growth. Startups must prioritize ruthlessly and resist distraction to execute those activities effectively.

3. **Consider both content and context.** You rarely need to re-create the wheel, but it is also dangerous to "lift and shift" practices from another organization to your own. Common practices within the startup community, for instance, are often driven by misguided "keeping up with Joneses" motivations. You need to construct a highly coherent and well-aligned set of people and management practices, modestly tailored to fit your organization.

Have a Plan

This can be a surprisingly difficult and controversial idea for startup leaders to accept. When change is occurring at a rapid pace and there is too much to do in the moment, leaders often avoid planning exercises. "We don't have time to think through that right now" is a common refrain. "We'll put together a plan after doing [XYZ]." The lack of time is merely a convenient excuse. Our experience suggests that startup leaders lack confidence in their ability to forecast and fear publicly stating goals that they may not meet, which in turn reduces their motivation to plan.

The discomfort in planning that startup leaders feel typically originates from not knowing where to start or their unsurprising preference to focus on other aspects of the business in which they are more knowledgeable. Yet, by choosing not to make conscious decisions related to people practices, that leader is indeed making an important decision—and usually a poor one. Peter Clarke, talent partner at Accel (a Palo Alto–based VC firm with $3 billion under management), says that "having a plan is crucial. Start by mapping a plan to things you understand. If you can think about your product road map, you can think about a people road map. Break it down into manageable tasks and execute on those tasks. Of course, your plan will change over time, but if you have a road map, you can get started."

Growing organizations inevitably add staff, shift people between teams, and allocate talent to mission-critical projects. Absent a plan, people are misplaced in roles, under- and overutilized, and often find themselves working in ways that do not support the organization's aims. Yes, plans will change. Yes, it will take time that could be spent writing code, interviewing candidates, or meeting with investors. However, putting together a people plan does not mean the business needs to be shut down for months at a time. Planning during a high-growth period is rarely a lengthy or overly formal process (you will never get things exactly right!), but the best leaders realize that planning needs to be a thoughtful and recurring process. Remember, if you do things right, your organization will continue to change, reaching a new stage of growth and complexity just when you feel you are starting to figure out the last stage!

Master (Only) the Basics

We believe that your core people programs should be well executed, well aligned, and mutually supportive at every stage of your company's evolution. Although the areas you address in a people plan will be relatively consistent, the number and types of programs you select should change as you evolve. We will point out "the basics" of each category for early-stage startups (generally, seed through Series B, and perhaps into Series C).

As an example, a particularly common trap that many growing organizations fall into after receiving substantial funding is deploying capital too quickly by hiring people, creating new roles, and even establishing entire functions that they do not yet need. This trap has become even more common thanks in part to misinterpretations and overgeneralizations of Reid Hoffman and Chris Yeh's "blitzscaling" principles[12] (see table 1.1). Although there is an undeniable pressure to manage investor perception by deploying capital in ways that signal growth, successful leaders know how to spend wisely on human capital. They anticipate and prioritize the short-, medium-, and long-term needs of their company and work their plan, thinking about appropriate benchmarks for how quickly to add people, which people to add, and the optimal layers of management essential for avoiding reckless and costly headcount expansion. We offer frameworks in each of these areas to help leaders navigate risks more responsibly while still moving quickly.

You will undoubtedly notice that "the basics" exclude many popular activities and programs. Rest assured, this is intentional. Creative, committed, and visionary entrepreneurs are highly susceptible to being overly ambitious. Trying to do too much, too early, is just as dangerous as the reverse. The best leaders focus on the essentials and delay peripheral "nice to do" activities (often treating those bright shiny objects as poisoned apples). For instance, if your company does not have a well-considered core health benefits package, it is almost certainly too early to add legions of other perks,

Table 1.1
Our approach versus blitzscaling

Blitzscaling	Our Approach	Normal Rules of Business
Make rapid guesstimates	Have a plan and rapidly revise it	Careful planning
Make inefficient investments	Invest in executing your plan	Cautious investment
Let small fires burn	Master (only) the basics	Solve all problems

Note: There is strong synergy with, as well as potential friction between, our "master the basics" concept and Hoffman and Yeh's blitzscaling principles. We agree that costs, competitors, and markets are uncertain for early-stage companies and that uncertainty should not drive an all-or-nothing choice between speed and efficiency. Only a few moonshot companies with rare runaway products and the deepest of pockets can get away with highly inefficient investments, and it only makes sense to blitzscale when you have determined that speed into the market is *the* critical strategy to achieve massive outcomes. The rest of the startup community will benefit most from making rapid, but high-quality decisions. Hoffman and Yeh acknowledge this point, highlighting that startups should navigate risks responsibly. So unless your business plan clearly meets Hoffman and Yeh's criteria for a blitzscaling business, we implore you to move quickly in accordance with a plan (which is both flexible and frequently revised). For many businesses, there is no need to increase the level of difficulty and likelihood of failure by racing without a map, with your eyes closed, while leaking fuel.

programs, and vendors. If you do not have stable company goals, it is too soon to implement individual bonus plans. And if you do not have experienced managers in place, you are probably not ready to start an internship program or emphasize campus hiring. The more priorities and programs your organization tries to tackle, the more challenging it becomes to deliver on them organizations are more likely to move three things a (figurative) mile than thirty things an inch. As your organization matures, you will be able to handle more elaborate people practices (and more sophisticated programs are likely to be necessary), but in your formative phases, you should strive to keep things simple for as long as possible.

A related reason that we emphasize mastering *only* the basics is that your employees have finite time, attention, and tolerance for distraction. If priorities change too quickly, or if there are too many people programs, employees either stop paying attention or get burned out trying to keep up with it all. Even if you can raise more money to overcome a blunder, you can never get back the time, attention, and opportunity cost that your team members wasted on a no longer relevant priority or noncore activity. Time is the ultimate nonrenewable resource, and it needs to be valued and protected fiercely. Similarly, trust and confidence in leadership can only be stretched so far. You can get more life out of the limited well of grace your employees are willing to extend to you after inevitable missteps by avoiding unforced errors in your people management programs.

Finally, as we discuss the basics, we will at times (and very selectively) suggest a specific tool, technology, or provider. This comes with notable risk because tools, technology, and even providers can become obsolete very quickly. We have consciously avoided emergent offerings that have not yet been adequately tested, and we hope you consider our referrals only as a starting point in your search rather than as an excuse to skirt due diligence.

Consider Content and Context

The chapter structure of this book lays out the essential content areas your people plan should encompass. We are confident that the high-level lessons can apply to any startup pursuing rapid growth. In many cases, you can avoid "re-creating the wheel" by using an established framework, tactic, or other resource when putting our lessons into practice. In this spirit, we reference numerous leaders in the high-growth community, consultants, and academic research that can help you shape your people plan. That said, our suggestions should not be considered a substitute for your own critical thinking. As you read and think about applying our suggestions, do not lose sight of the context in which your current situation is embedded.

You need to select the best tools for the chosen purpose rather than applying tactics that worked for someone else solving a (sometimes subtly) different problem. For example, you may find a better way to meet the underlying criteria of effective performance management *in your organization* than simply adopting an exemplar practice described in our book. Our point is not to diminish the value of these lessons but to encourage you to focus on the *why* (e.g., understanding how and why high-level principles lead to better performance management) more than the *what* (e.g., what specific HR platform should be used to administer performance management reviews) of the lessons. Millions and millions of dollars have been wasted by purchasing unnecessary people management software, implementing lavish perk programs, or mandating specific candidate selection processes that do not fit a specific business.

Extending this perspective, as you think about which programs you might want to implement, remember the adage "correlation is not causation." Many unicorns are already major name brands and have such a strong product or business model that they can achieve a large measure of success *despite* their management practices. In fact, research suggests

Table 1.2
Do's and don't do's of a strong people strategy

Don't Do—Examples	Do Instead—Examples
Use anecdotal evidence to create pay packages (XYZ told me they make $$$, so we should . . .).	Obtain a compensation benchmarking report from a reputable organization.
Mirror the health benefits package of big tech companies such as Google, Facebook, or Uber.	Work with your benefit broker to determine a market-appropriate package for your company.
Create all your job descriptions from scratch (and watch them go out of date almost immediately).	Edit from the template of benchmarking reports and competitor job postings.
Create your own "how to be a good manager" training materials.	Adapt resources from a reputable organization that align with your leadership team's values.
Set your engineers to the task of coding your own applicant tracking system.	Sign up for a subscription to an existing platform from a short list of well-known vendors.

that bad management practices prevail all the time—and they are usually rooted in faulty attributions based on early "luck" events or someone's first- or secondhand experience at an altogether different firm.[13] Consider these examples: Google gave equity to cafeteria workers; Zappos eliminated managerial roles entirely; and the founder/CEO of Southwest Airlines reportedly drank quarts of Wild Turkey on the job during the airline's early days.[14] These companies went on to great success, but probably despite rather than as a result of these practices. You will, inevitably, hear of an innovative practice at another startup and feel tempted to follow suit. We urge extreme caution (see table 1.2). The lessons in this book provide time-tested, evidence-based strategies anchored in practical applications and presented in plain talk so you can do what is best for your company at your current stage.

When Should You Apply These Lessons?

The need to update management practices is triggered by increasing complexity within the organization, which is usually the product of more employees, more layers of management, and increasing dispersion of talent. If the complexity in your organization feels overwhelming, you are not alone. Scholars exploring a broad range of phenomena consistently assert that challenges grow exponentially (not linearly) as headcounts expand.[15] Our experience suggests that there are significant transition points around twenty employees

Table 1.3
Common headcount thresholds

0–20 employees	~20–50	~50–100	~100+
Seed stage	Series A	Series B	Series C
Crisis of leadership		Crisis of autonomy	

and again at around one hundred employees. Those employee counts map roughly to the typical timing of funding rounds, as shown in table 1.3.

Larry Greiner, former business school professor (University of Southern California) and management expert, developed an extremely helpful framework of "evolution and revolution" for thinking about organizational change.[16] We draw from this framework to illustrate our points about startup transition (see figure 1.3). Greiner first argued that a founder's creativity and entrepreneurial drive are the key factors in early-stage startup success but that these startups eventually (we argue at about twenty employees) experience a *crisis of leadership*. At this point, founders find themselves burdened with management responsibilities that they are unprepared to carry, and employees are no longer persuaded merely by the founder's communications. To survive, organizations must implement mechanisms that provide clear direction and focus throughout the organization, which often goes against the founder's preference for what has worked in the past.

The next critical juncture for startups is a *crisis of autonomy*, which we argue occurs at around one hundred employees. At this point, process and structure have usually evolved so that clear functional groups exist (e.g., marketing, engineering), budgets and policies are institutionalized, and communication is more regimented and less personal. Although these practices align employee efforts with company priorities, they tend to be highly centralized and create problematic bottleneck problems around a few senior leaders. To continue a successful evolution, organizations must make changes that push decision-making authority down in the hierarchy. This is particularly challenging because it goes against existing leaders' preferences or habits toward directive styles and is likewise jarring to staff who are not used to, or trained for, more critical decision-making.

Rather than make the shift with good planning and intentionality (i.e., hiring more experienced staff, training and educating existing staff, or creating a system of checks and balances to allow delegation with less risk), many startups hold on to their centralized approach and end up losing

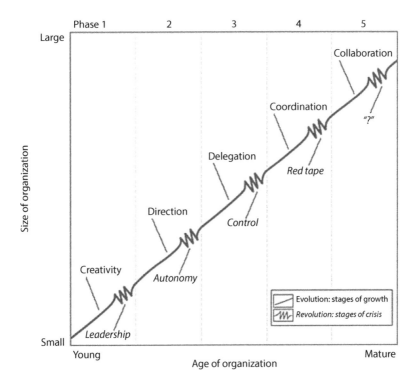

Figure 1.3
Greiner's five phases of growth
Source: Permission granted by HBSP; Greiner, "Evolution and Revolution as Organizations Grow," *Harvard Business Review*, May–June 1998.

talented employees who were looking for more growth and responsibility. As growth continues to 150+ employees, companies experience new challenges due to diminishing trust and weaker personal relationships.[17] And so the cycle of evolution and revolution continues.

Start thinking about your people plan now, but know going in that this will be a recurring, evolutionary process. Indeed, appropriate practices at one stage of evolution often result in major challenges at the next stage (i.e., "the solution creates the problem"). Although initially a frustrating sentiment, leaders who have experience in multiple startups will tell you that sometimes a breakdown is just another sign of positive growth ("if things aren't breaking, you're not growing"). Our general rule of thumb is to plan on revisions around significant funding events, or every eighteen months, whichever comes first.

How Is This Book Organized?

This book addresses specific aspects of the overall web of people practices. Each chapter begins with an introduction to the chapter topic penned by an expert in that functional area. This is followed by a brief outline of the content presented under the three major headings: "The Problem" facing startups; "The Plan" that we recommend; and "The Basics" that startup leaders should understand in this area. This work is not intended to be a story, so don't feel that you need to read through this book cover to cover. We intend this work to act as a reference guide and a practical resource. Table 1.4 provides a quick overview of each chapter.

Table 1.4
Key lessons by chapter

Chapter	Topic	Key Lessons
1	Scaling for Success	• High growth companies have special but predictable needs • Have a plan • Master (only) the basics • Consider both content and context
2	Organizational Structure: Designing a Framework for Growth	• Aim for the Goldilocks zone (not too much or too little structure and control) • Ensure structure enables decision-making • Hire stage-appropriate leaders • Maintain management spans and layers
3	Talent Acquisition: Building a Team to Propel Growth	• Create a workforce plan • Clearly define the roles to fill • Build a candidate generation engine • Construct a recruitment team • Use effective selection processes
4	Total Rewards: Creating a Compelling Employment Value Proposition	• Offer competitive cash and core health benefits • Be selective about additional perks and programs • Create an equity ownership plan • Clarify the employment value proposition
5	Learning and Development: Core and Strategic Investments	• Invest in the common core offerings • Layer in only a few high-impact programs • Say "no" or "not yet" to everything else • Measure the impact • Determine execution strategy

6	Culture, Engagement, and Communications: Creating the Environment for Success	• Honor the best of the past while embracing the future • Define a clear and differentiated culture • Be yourself • Align programs to support your desired culture • Ensure good two-way communication
7	Performance Management and Goal Setting: Clarity, Consistency, and Consequences	• Set simple and clear goals • Provide effective feedback • Create consequences that matter
8	Legal and Compliance: Common Traps and Easy Answers	• Standardize most employment practices • Establish compliant wage-hour policies and practices • Set up compliant accommodation policies
9	How and When to Construct Your People Team: Supporting Your Scale-Up	• Manage to what matters • Keep it simple for as long as possible • Look out for key transition points • Quickly solve for payroll and benefits delivery • Grab the reins of recruitment • In-source specialist support as you scale
10	Where Next?	• Plan ahead • Drive focus and clarity • Pick great advisors • Communicate openly and often • Lead change—don't fight it

Conclusion

Our professional experiences, consulting work, teaching, and research convinced us that startup leaders need an evidence-based roadmap that is easily accessible and highly practical. In that spirit, we have integrated management research with interesting, boots-on-the-ground examples and lessons from many of today's (and tomorrow's) most respected leaders and organizations. Although academically rigorous and built on scholarly principles, this is not designed to be a classroom textbook. Our work focuses directly on the unique tensions and challenges that rapidly growing organizations face and the people practices necessary to navigate those choppy waters. We are confident that the lessons in this book will resonate with anyone eager to understand how to more effectively steer an organization through rapid growth.

2

Organizational Structure

Designing a Framework for Growth

Here is the thing: there is no "right" organizational structure. But! When we have organization-wide problems (morale, dysfunction, lack of urgency, execution problems, etc.), we look to the organization chart with a belief that therein lies the problem. "We need to change this org model." Moving from a business unit to a functional model. Moving from a functional model to a regional model. From centralization to decentralization. Or vice versa. We believe that designing a "better" model, and then effectively shepherding the change necessary to get there, will yield the improvement we need. Maybe it will— or maybe what you see in the following months is simply a temporary Hawthorne effect.

Employees are pessimistic about any new organization structure. They'll have heard this story before. "Here we go—more org changes." They'll believe the pendulum will eventually swing to a new organization—perhaps back to the way it was done even before the change! Any change for employees—even if positive—will typically elicit a SARAH cycle effect, where they're first sad about having to report to a new boss, then angry, then rejecting it, then eventually accepting and happy. But for these reasons and others, the desired end results from an organizational change often do not materialize.

An organization structure—and a changed structure—is simply one tool to arrive at the desired outcomes (and are those even clear from the onset?). For the problem being solved for, let's say, stronger cohesion across team A + B, an organizational structure will only be effective if all the other necessary components are present: strong leadership, coherent culture/values, strong governance, and ongoing efforts to improve the team dynamic. Said another way, you could have a horribly incoherent organizational structure—but with those other things present, perhaps the organizational structure problems are barely visible! When solving for a problem with organizational structure, it can't simply be thought of as a problem in isolation.

—DAVID HANRAHAN, CHRO AT EVENTBRITE AND
FORMER VP OF PEOPLE AT NIANTIC AND ZENDESK

CHAPTER 2 RUNDOWN

The Problem
As your organization adds workers, complexity increases exponentially.

The Plan
Design structures that define role boundaries, reduce conflict, and clarify decision-making rights.

The Basics
1. Aim for the Goldilocks zone (not too much or too little structure/control).
2. Ensure structure enables decision-making.
3. Hire stage-appropriate leaders.
4. Maintain appropriate management spans and layers.

The Problem

For a startup, increasing your organization's headcount is important for two reasons. First, from an operational perspective, you need more workers when you acquire new customers and begin to wrestle with the many challenges your company will face. After all, you and your team have probably been working at an unsustainable pace for too long, so the status quo is no longer viable. Second, increasing your headcount can serve as a positive signal to investors that their capital is being meaningfully deployed in the time period before tangible results materialize. To drive growth and value creation (versus just increasing costs), you need a thoughtful and intentional operating model to guide employee expansion. That operating model is your *organizational structure*; it determines the divisions of labor, coordinates patterns within and across functions/positions, establishes lines of authority, and specifies the decision-making rights in the company.

In our undergraduate and MBA classes, students typically assume that as long as an organization's key products/services and processes work, the organization will be able to propel growth simply by hiring more people and stubbornly resisting change (e.g., if three salespeople can generate $3 million per year, then six people should be able to bring in $6 million). To the untrained eye, scaling up is primarily a replication exercise. But, experienced leaders know that the relationship between headcount and growth is neither straightforward nor linear. Adding employees dramatically increases the complexity of an organization[1] and, somewhat ironically, can make rapid growth more difficult.[2] Designing a structure that works is a major differentiator between a headcount expansion that fuels exponential growth and one that produces growth-destroying inefficiencies and dysfunctions.

The Plan

Before searching another job board, soliciting another employee referral, or fielding another applicant phone call, you must find time to critically evaluate the organizational structure that works best for your organization. Your organization's structure is its architecture. Research strongly indicates that choices regarding organizational structure have a meaningful impact on the success of new ventures,[3] and in this spirit, Brad Kirkman (a chaired business school professor at North Carolina State University) told us that "a good design can cover for imperfect management, but even perfect managers will fail to overcome a bad design."

Organizational structures range from tall hierarchies to flat holocracies, rigid bureaucracies to empowering systems, and so on. In most cases, startups that want to scale rapidly start with loose, flat structures that offer a great deal of flexibility at the expense of more uncertainty and less focus.[4] More mature firms, by contrast, often have multiple layers of formal hierarchy to oversee specialized roles, trading some flexibility for greater efficiency, control, and predictability. These contrasting approaches highlight an important and particularly challenging dynamic for leaders at high-growth organizations: As firms mature, the downsides of a flat, egalitarian structure become more pronounced, and a once-acceptable trade-off is no longer sustainable. Consistent with the "What got you here won't get you there" mantra from Chapter 1, Jim Chrisman and colleagues write that "the structural attributes that increase the probability of a venture's success may decrease its probability of survival."[5] In other words, successful firms effectively transition from a relatively informal structure early on (as they sort out common startup problems) to a more formalized structure as they grow.[6]

Although intuitive in principle, knowing when and how to transition from a relatively informal structure to a more formal structure can be difficult when you are in the moment. For most growing startups, things are happening fast, and even reasonable structural changes are seen as major threats by employees—and often by founders. Ranjay Gulati (Harvard) and Alicia DeSantola (University of Washington) astutely note that formally defining roles and establishing hierarchy are often seen as "bureaucratic threats to their [founders'] entrepreneurial souls."[7] Similarly, the late sociologist Max Weber referred to organizational bureaucracies as "iron cages" used to control employees![8] Although a well-defined structure will create some trade-offs, rest assured that it does not have to compromise *all* of the good aspects of your company's culture. Case in point: The U.S. Navy—an unquestionably hierarchical and bureaucratic organization—is famous for several successful empowerment initiatives,[9] and even Google learned (the hard way) that employees prefer having a manager to "disorganization."[10] A final word of caution before we move on: If you don't create a structure of your own design, your employees will do so on their own.[11] *And there is no guarantee they will pick a good one.*

Four basic principles can guide you toward an optimal structure for your organization's growth ambitions, and we discuss them in the following section.

The Basics

Basic 1: Aim for the Goldilocks zone (not too much or too little structure/control)

Which structure is best for your organization? As with most questions in the fields of organizational behavior and management science, the answer is a resounding "it depends."[12] Do not despair, this uncertainty need not be overwhelming. We concur with the observations of Elad Gil (entrepreneur, author, and advisor to several leading companies), who notes that deciding on an organizational structure is, at its core, an exercise in deciding who will break ties (e.g., who will make decisions) and which trade-offs are most palatable in your organization.[13] We further echo Gil's advice that you should not stress about finding the *perfect* structure so much as worry about finding *one* structure that works for your organization for the next few months (because successful growth means your company will soon need to restructure again). To that end, leaders should aim to find a structure that is in a general range (i.e., the Goldilocks zone) of suitability for the next twelve months.

A number of indicators can suggest when a startup needs to institute more structure, including unclear or overlapping roles, increased miscommunication, and general confusion among employees (for other examples, see table 2.1). One reason these issues manifest stems from the practice of bringing in new employees and managers without a clear idea of what those individuals will do. In the absence of a reality check or a strong senior leader to ensure broad and consistent alignment with organizational priorities, chaos will ensue. Some groups will strive to build empires by vastly overhiring, creating unnecessary bureaucracy and inflating cash burn rate. Other groups will descend into functional infighting, advocating for their team's priorities without having a clear picture of what is most important to the larger organization. Many inexperienced leaders take a "wait and hope" approach, thinking that employees will be able to figure out goals and priorities on their own. This approach relies on faulty and outright dangerous assumptions. Every time an individual employee or unit decides to do something, the organization itself is simultaneously making a decision *not* to use its time and talent on something else.

Would your teams get more done if they knew what they should be working on and how it fit into the bigger picture, received regular feedback, and knew what resources they had to work with? For many startups at the early stages of growth, the answer is "probably." However, it is difficult for startup leaders to have a broad enough perspective to accurately self-assess these situations, and your team is unlikely to bring these issues to your attention before they reach a boiling point. An external coach, a trusted advisor, or a partner who is not experiencing the same stress

Table 2.1
Common indicators of a structure that is under- or overcontrolling

Undercontrolling	Overcontrolling
• Job titles or job descriptions do not exist or are poorly defined. • Some employees have multiple direct or dotted-line managers. • It is unclear who breaks ties, allocates resources, or determines priorities across teams—or the person who makes those decisions is not readily accessible. • There are a high number of direct reports for a given manager, particularly when those direct reports span multiple functions or disciplines. • Teams or individuals are working on potentially conflicting projects. • Deadlines are being missed and costs are regularly running above expectations. • A senior leader actively avoids engagement in an area that they are responsible for because he or she does not have deep subject matter expertise. • Performance feedback for individuals and teams is limited or inconsistent.	• There is a high span of control (# of direct reports per manager) and relatively few layers of management in the organization. • The CEO directly manages more than 5–6 departments or functional leaders. • There are more than 3 hours of recurring senior leadership meetings per month (often called "planning meetings") • Meetings with the CEO are often unscheduled or unplanned. • The CEO takes questions directly to staff members rather than involving the functional or department leader (a "fly-by"). • Strategic direction changes or major business priorities change with minimal explanation or context.

can provide a good reality check on your organizational effectiveness. Once diagnosed, you can apply some straightforward solutions, which we outline in table 2.2.

The other end of the spectrum (i.e., too much structure and control) is also fraught with risk. Problems with overstructuring can arise from many issues in organizations (e.g., too many layers, overly bureaucratic processes), but in high-growth organizations they most commonly center around a founder or CEO who wants to be a highly centralized figure in too much of the organization's inner workings and decision-making. Naturally directive leaders, especially when under pressure, tend to intensify their controlling behaviors and often implement structures that reflect this preference. Even the most brilliant and low-ego leaders can quickly morph into micromanagers in stressful times. Founders and entrepreneurs working

Table 2.2
Common remedies for not enough or too much structure/control

General tips for calibrating your structure

- Document and share the goals for the company as a whole.
- Document and share goals for each major department and function.
- Document and share the core roles and responsibilities for each major function (i.e., product, engineering, marketing, sales, etc.).
- Clearly identify the primary decision-maker for each significant organizational unit and ensure that those individuals are actively engaged.
- Ensure that all managers of people are conducting team meetings and one-on-ones at least every month.
- Evaluate and adjust management spans of control and the number of management layers in each major group.
- Evaluate existing senior leadership and implement plans to help them develop their skills. This may include training, executive coaching, layering, or replacement as needed.
- Set up a communication cadence for the entire organization, with all-hands updates occurring at least quarterly.

Remedies for not enough structure

- Clearly identify how decisions will be made that cross organizational boundaries (i.e., those that impact multiple functions, divisions, or geographies).
- Establish company-level goal prioritization, headcount planning, and budgeting processes.
- Evaluate existing senior leadership, and implement plans to help them develop their skills. This may include training, executive coaching, layering, or replacing them as needed.

Remedies for too much structure

- Consider using a broader "executive council" to make decisions if the CEO or another senior leader is solely responsible for all issues that cross organizational boundaries (i.e., impact product, engineering, and finance).
- Set up a lightweight cross-functional project status reporting process (reducing CEO fly-bys).
- Shield the CEO from a high volume of ad hoc requests by redefining the delegation of authority.
- Ensure any leaders exhibiting overly controlling behaviors receive specific and timely feedback.

within a rapidly scaling business frequently fall into this trap as they struggle to adapt to the changing needs of their business. Leaders of small companies are accustomed to being aware of everything that occurs in their organization, and they expect to be able to directly make things happen through their personal effort, intellect, and force of will. These leaders commonly take too much on themselves, centralize decision-making, mandate frequent check-ins with their team, and come up with creative excuses for not vesting managers with more autonomy and authority.

Unfortunately, control-heavy approaches quickly become nonviable in an organization with multiple layers of management, geographic dispersion, and numerous competing priorities. Even if a founder/leader is absolutely tireless and incredibly brilliant, it is simply unrealistic and grossly inefficient for a single leader to be highly competent in operations, sales, human resources, product, marketing, finance, accounting, technology, and all the other functions of a growing business. Leaders of rapidly growing businesses *should* be engaged in every decision of major importance, but they should also actively avoid creating unnecessary bottlenecks around every single decision. Indicators that your organization is operating with too much structure or control are highlighted in table 2.1.

How can you remedy a situation in which the organization has too much structure and a senior leader is exhibiting controlling behaviors? The first step is recognizing it, of course. However, similar to our previous comments, self-assessment is difficult, and knowing exactly where the line should be drawn is often a contentious discussion. Further complicating matters, even senior managers under the watch of a controlling leader may be reluctant to speak up truthfully (this is more of an issue when a controlling leader is at the helm versus when there is too little structure). At large organizations, assessment and intervention are often performed by an internal senior HR leader, but smaller organizations usually lack people with the experience and independence to make this call. Therefore, the best way to diagnose an overly structured environment is often to engage an external advisor who can observe the leader in action and take the temperature of the team as an unbiased third party. This will require the CEO's visible support to be optimally successful, but the external advisor can usually gather more honest feedback from team members and suggest changes in ways that allow the CEO to save face. We have provided a short list of potential remedies for overcoming problems of too much structure in table 2.2.

Organizational structure decisions play a big role in influencing the overall capability of a company and are critical to its success. It can be difficult to diagnose your own situation, particularly if leadership has not worked within a wide variety of contexts and environments. Trusted team members and third-party advisors can be invaluable in determining opportunities for improvement. As you evaluate next steps for your organization, be careful not to overcorrect. Keep in mind there is value in both moderating an executive's behavior to allow for more employee freedom and maintaining the ability for an executive to keep team members accountable. If you decide a change is needed, we concur with author and consultant Elad Gil's advice to be thorough in your planning (i.e., know where everyone will land); get buy-in from key stakeholders before the roll out; communicate clearly and compassionately; and act quickly when executing the reorganization.[14]

Basic 2: Ensure structure enables decision-making

An ideal structure maximizes coordination and control of your employees, but it also sets the stage for them to do their best work. Two of the most important characteristics of a good structure are *high role clarity* (i.e., specifying the tasks and responsibilities of a given position) and *minimal role conflict* (i.e., ensuring expectations are consistent and compatible with one another). When functional boundaries are clear and do not conflict, you can more efficiently coordinate your employees' efforts toward the most important organizational goals and more precisely diagnose and remedy problems (e.g., holding employees accountable for their performance, monitoring unit progress, and quickly identifying problems in the overall system).[15] Increased role clarity and reduced role conflict also improve the employee experience. Research indicates that clearer and less conflicting roles are associated with lower levels of employee anxiety and higher levels of satisfaction, commitment, and performance.[16] In other words, good fences often make good neighbors.

Designing an effective organizational structure requires thoughtful consideration not only on narrow, interdepartmental issues that hinder role clarity and conflict for a particular position but also on broader, system-level issues related to how each function and role connects with other roles and functions (e.g., reporting lines, team assignments). The importance of, and challenge behind, establishing clear roles that do not conflict is magnified in periods of high growth. In these periods, new roles and lines of reporting are constantly being created; newcomers are struggling to figure out how they can and should contribute; and tenured employees are frequently asked to modify their tasks and responsibilities (sometimes against their wishes). In short, chaos abounds, and in the absence of a meaningful structure, it becomes nearly impossible to determine who is doing what and how decisions will be made. As a result, some key tasks are unnecessarily completed by multiple employees and teams (the redundancy problem), and other tasks are not being done by *anyone.* In these situations, employees quickly grow frustrated and lose confidence in management.

A thorough and thoughtful exercise in mapping the boundaries between each major function or role can reduce these pains significantly, but keep in mind that it is possible to have too much of a good thing. Speaking to this issue, Steve McElfresh, former chief human resources officer (CHRO) of New Relic and an experienced HR consultant in Silicon Valley, told us that he encourages his clients to strive for "almost enough structure," the implied message being that identifying a few key responsibilities is in many cases superior to lengthy checklists of tasks, duties, and responsibilities that will quickly become outdated. We agree. In fact, one of the most common setbacks we see occurs when well-intentioned leaders create overly detailed and specific roles that breed interdepartmental conflicts and reduce employees' willingness to be adaptable. A related problem is that a tremendous amount of time and effort from multiple stakeholders is required to create these roles, which in turn means that they are rarely updated as the business evolves. Erring on the light side of specific role definitions allows you to update priorities more frequently and preserves the ability for your employees to react appropriately to changing environments. Rather than creating multipage job descriptions that are out of date almost immediately and are rarely referenced, we encourage clients to utilize a simple RACI (an acronym for responsible, accountable, consulted, informed) chart (table 2.3).

Table 2.3
RACI template

Activity	Responsible	Accountable	Consulted	Informed
Source job candidates	Recruiting team	Hiring manager	Department head; recruiting manager	Tracked in Greenhouse applicant tracking system
Set compensation ranges for new jobs	Director of total rewards	Senior vice president of people	Department heads	Hiring managers; financial planning and analysis
New hire onboarding week	Training team	Hiring manager	Department head	Status tracked by training team
New hire access and equipment setup	IT operations	Hiring manager	Department head	Status tracked by IT operations

The RACI chart is simple to adapt and apply. Identifying the largest areas of confusion and deciding (then documenting and publicizing) who is responsible for a particular issue can provide valuable clarity and resolve unnecessary conflict and distraction within an organization. Many excellent online resources provide free information and guidance for using a RACI chart effectively.[17]

Basic 3: Hire stage-appropriate leaders

One of the most important—and challenging—activities for a startup founder is building out the leadership team. As discussed in the previous section, you will need to do some (but not too much) hiring in anticipation of future needs. As part of your efforts, you will probably hire a number of functional leaders and middle managers with critical experience and expertise that your organization lacks. An all too common problem in many startups is that more senior employees (CEOs, founders, etc.) impede—passively or actively, unintentionally or intentionally—the ability of new leaders to grow the organization. These challenges often involve personnel issues that can be mitigated with the right approach.

Carmela Krantz, founder of WovenHR and nine-time top HR leader, says, "trust the leaders you hire to do the jobs you hired them to do. Create a process that works for you to set expectations and check in on progress. Then set an expectation that members of the leadership team will work collaboratively and not need to have the CEO/founder be a part of every meeting or decision." In some cases, new leaders are brought in with the explicit expectation that they will build or reshape their teams. This is ideal in several ways, but in other cases this will not be possible. One such instance occurs when you need to grow part of a team before you hire the formal leader of that team. You may, for example, hire several software engineers before your organization needs a full-time chief technology officer (CTO). In other cases, you may have bookended your hires with a senior leader (CTO) and front-line employees (software engineers), bringing in mid-level managers later to handle ever-expanding day-to-day activities. In both scenarios, newly hired managers of people are inheriting previously tenured team members and their histories rather than being the new manager's own handpicked, "blank slate" employees. These leaders, unsurprisingly, face a litany of potential challenges that can impede their ability to get things done.[18]

To set your new leaders up for maximum success, focus on hiring a "player/coach" as your first hire in most new departments or functions. This is a particularly relevant approach for early-stage startups at seed or Series A rounds. A player/coach is skilled and humble enough to directly perform the transactional work from day one but also is experienced enough to lead a small group as the department grows. The ideal career level for someone like this is somewhere within the senior manager, director, and senior director range. You should openly talk with a prospective player/coach about how the role's functional breadth will eventually grow to the point that a more senior leader (vice president or above) may be hired above them. You can then allow the player/coach to develop a functional strategy and select team members. When the time to hire a more senior leader comes, involve the player/coach in the selection process. The effort you invest in setting appropriate expectations and engaging the player/coach in the senior leader search process is vital to a smooth transition and the new leader's success.

Another frequent challenge occurs when well-liked early hires—who are usually responsible for a major part of the organization's past success—are faced with the prospect of being layered (i.e., being placed under a previously nonexistent manager) or altogether removed from the organization. In this scenario, you can expect to hear all kinds of rationalizations from the CEO, cofounders, and department heads for why the early employee should be protected. Typically, this takes the form of impassioned speeches about disrupting the organization's culture or "sending the wrong signal." In more extreme cases, senior stakeholders will drag their feet on budget allocations and approvals for new hires. These situations are incredibly distracting and detrimental to a new leader's efforts to build a team. Although we certainly agree that culture and budget controls are important concerns, they should not be manipulated as a way to avoid making the best personnel decision available. Keeping a suboptimal employee around or even providing a one-off reporting line to top management to honor past contributions undermines your structure and sends a terrible message to new leaders.

Speaking to this danger, Elad Gil writes, "if you start making exceptions for the squeakiest wheels, you may reverse the whole reason you are making the change, as well as show people you are open to being politicked."[19] Saydeah Howard, chief talent officer at IVP, expanded on this point when she told us this:

> The trap I see most often is companies "settling" for someone who is okay because there's a pressing business need, versus waiting to find the great candidate. They often think having someone, anyone, in the role is better than taking the risk to wait. This trap leads to a lot of

wrong people being in positions they shouldn't [have] and staying in roles significantly longer than they should. Which is the other trap I see startups falling into—not recognizing when the company has outgrown someone. Very few people can stretch from the early days of a startup, fighting for the first few dollars of revenue, to the late-stage company with well over $100 million in revenue. As companies grow and face different challenges, individuals may not have the appropriate skill set or interest to continue growing with the organization. CEOs and leadership teams need to recognize that and make changes sooner rather than later. I've never heard a CEO say they moved out an executive too early but often hear that they regret not doing it sooner.

If you are unwilling to make tough decisions, you will inevitably handicap the potential of your organization. New managers quickly become disenfranchised when they receive too much pushback from senior leadership, so you must cede responsibility, power, and some degree of latitude in team design if you are serious about scaling successfully.

Basic 4: Maintain appropriate management spans and layers

When people think of organizational structures, they frequently envision an organizational chart illustrating the firm's hierarchy. This hierarchy generally highlights two aspects: *spans of control* (or just "spans"), showing the number of direct reports under a manager, and the number of management *layers* between executives and frontline employees. Managing spans and layers is critical to organizational functioning irrespective of company stage or maturity level, but this is an especially tricky process during rapid growth. Your efforts to hire ahead of current needs, accelerated and unpredictable workloads, and other unexpected events (e.g., market shifts, regulatory changes) can contribute to a hierarchy that quickly gets out of whack, as seen in figure 2.1.

As discussed in the previous section, sometimes functional managers are hired with the explicit expectation that they will design and build their teams from scratch. In these circumstances, the new manager's span of control will appear abnormally low during the departmental ramp-up, suggesting that the manager is being underutilized. After just a few months, however, the ratio of employees per manager can change dramatically to the point that the manager is overextended and making difficult trade-offs

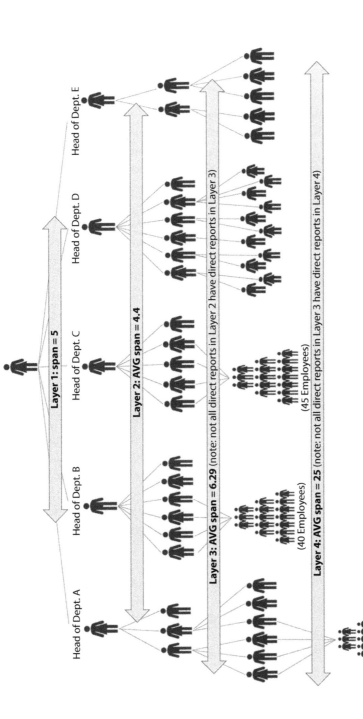

Figure 2.1
Spans and layers

between strategic and day-to-day operating activities. In a high-growth organization, a manager will need to play some part in the daily workflow and transactional processes as well as take on a significant amount of interpersonal leadership responsibilities. A substantial body of scholarly research suggests that managers can, and *should*, play a vital role in onboarding new hires,[20] so you should plan for appropriate managerial bandwidth in the months following significant hiring activity. As a guiding principle, spans should feel stretched but not to the point that it is impossible for managers to know their team members well and provide regular feedback.

Generally speaking, the optimal span of control decreases as the complexity of the role or function increases.[21] Very much related, spans should increase as you move down the hierarchy where more specialized and more similar multi-incumbent individual contributor roles exist (there are exceptions, of course; managing cross-functional activities can require more time). For example, a skilled leader could potentially manage a team of twenty or more employees holding similar transactional roles (e.g., warehouse, call center, or retail), whereas a CEO may only be able to realistically handle four to six direct reports given that each report is in charge of a complex unit. Ensuring appropriate spans of control, and thus maximizing the effectiveness of your managers, is a critical lever for your organization's scaling success. Yet time and time again we have seen organizations develop highly inefficient spans of control for any number of reasons.

Our decision to discuss spans before layers is intentional. When you make good decisions about spans, the right number of management layers usually becomes evident. A wise (and frugal) executive will delay adding a management layer until spans have clearly become unwieldy. The addition of each new layer of management creates an enormous overhead of complexity, coordination, and cost without any guarantee of added benefit. Thus erring on the side of compression is typically favorable to expansion when you are unsure that new layers will add value.

Too often in growing startups we see departments comprised of a single VP who manages one or two directors, who in turn each manage a handful of analysts. In these cases, the VP is typically pleased to delegate people management responsibilities to the directors while focusing upward on more strategic issues with the senior leadership team. But directors are less satisfied with this arrangement because they would prefer to have direct reporting lines to more senior executives for personal status, control, and efficiency reasons. This arrangement reflects a highly inefficient and difficult to maintain structure. If you were to flatten the organization by collapsing layers, or if you never added those layers in the first place (the preferable option), organizational effectiveness would likely improve.

Organizations will vary in terms of the "right" number of layers, but we can offer some general rules of thumb to guide your thinking. Until you reach about twenty employees, there are usually only two layers of management: the CEO and the staff. As you eclipse twenty employees, the first managers of people are usually hired, forming a new third layer of management. The fourth layer is added when department heads are brought in over those managers and report directly to the founders. That fourth layer can accommodate up to one hundred employees, depending on the size of any individual department. When your organization expands to five layers of management, complexity accelerates, and job titling and leveling distinctions take on greater importance. Table 2.4 illustrates this complexity.

Be vigilant in your efforts to expand spans and compress layers whenever possible. Even if you think everything is humming along just fine, take a formal inventory of the spans and layers within your organization *at least* once a year. You might be surprised at what you find! Unnecessary layers can quickly creep in if not monitored, which can lead to inefficient

Table 2.4
Factors influencing spans and layers

Factors	Relationship to Span	Relationship to Layers
Employee headcount	Not directly related	More headcount necessitates more layers
Contractors, temporary staff, vendors	Contingent workers absorb managerial capacity	Not directly related
Pace of growth	With faster growth, strive for reduced span	Not directly related
Business model complexity (channels, customers, products)	Business model complexity absorbs managerial capacity at senior levels	Not directly related
Nature of the work (specialized skills required)	Complex work absorbs managerial capacity	Minimize layers when possible in specialized groups
Geographic dispersion of staff	Dispersion absorbs managerial capacity	Not directly related
Potential Distractions:		
Revenue Funding (round, total raised) Industry	Not directly related	Not directly related

spans. What seemed complex at one point may become simple or perfunctory later as processes become refined and employees develop knowledge, skills, and routines. Thus the optimal spans and layers in your organization may need updating, even if the average number of direct reports has not changed dramatically.

Conclusion

One of the most important keys to success is helping senior executives shift their mindset and leadership styles to match the current stage of the organization, be it a sole entrepreneur, a team, or a team of teams. As the leadership requirements expand, executives must surround themselves with team members who are willing to create and empower a structure that optimizes the coordination, control, and clarity within and between roles. We acknowledge that this is not easy, and it will be nearly impossible to objectively arrive at the perfect balance between holding people accountable versus micromanagement, empowering employees versus abdicating responsibility, and stretching spans versus overwhelming managers. Yet with genuine self-reflection, forethought, and often the help of trusted advisors, you can move closer to the Goldilocks zone where your business will thrive.

3

Talent Acquisition

Building a Team to Propel Growth

In my recruitment leadership roles during the early days at Instacart, Uber, Salesforce, and Apple in both the United States and Japan, I lived in the every day is a crisis startup environment. One of the most important things that growing companies can do is to have a plan around their growth—a workforce plan. Why are they adding headcount? What are those new employees expected to deliver? What will those people do? It's vital to have clear expectations for each role, avoiding confusion, overlaps, and hiring for the wrong spec. If you don't know that you're getting the right people to fill the current need, it's likely that time, money, and effort will all be wasted. Good workforce planning really matters—which should be a collaboration between recruitment, finance, and people operations.

Then you need to figure out who the right people are. Too many hiring managers rely on gut feel interviews. In my experience, the people who feel the most comfortable using an informal interview are the worst at effectively assessing hires. Especially when you're hiring a lot of people, you need to have a structured interview and a well-defined selection process, with a clear decision-making rubric. That's because inexperienced managers, which startups are full of, tend to be afraid to make a mistake and are slow to pull the trigger on making a hire.

Hiring is one of the largest challenges for high-growth companies. The founders need to adjust their level of

involvement, require the hiring managers to take ownership for the process, and empower them to make more
decisions. Otherwise everything gets bottlenecked.

—MICHAEL J. CASE, CEO AT NEPTUNE PEOPLE, FORMER
HEAD OF TALENT ACQUISITION FOR INSTACART, UBER
AMERICAS OPERATIONS, SALESFORCE JAPAN, AND
APPLE JAPAN

CHAPTER 3 RUNDOWN

The Problem
You know you need more people, but you don't know how many or where to
    find them.

The Plan
Map your needs, and build a step-by-step talent acquisition strategy.

The Basics
1. Create a workforce (hiring) plan, predicting your needs.
2. Clearly define the roles to fill.
3. Build a candidate generation engine.
4. Construct a recruitment team.
5. Use effective selection processes.

The Problem

After designing the right structure for your organization (chapter 2), you
face the challenge of filling out that structure with the team members you
need to effectively grow. Successfully building your team requires thoughtful *workforce planning* and *talent acquisition* strategies. Workforce planning
refers to the ongoing process of determining exactly what you need, where
you need it, and when you need it. It is, in essence, the bridge between
your organizational structure and successful talent acquisition efforts. Your
talent acquisition strategies determine how you will go about executing
your workforce plan. Effective talent acquisition boils down to finding the
right people (high quality), at the right time (quickly), at the right price
(compensation within selected market range).

Finding and acquiring the right talent is an extremely critical part of any business and has consequently burgeoned into a competitive, expensive[1] game that many leaders in high-growth environments are forced to learn on the fly. Peter Clarke, a talent partner at Accel, told us, "If you were to ask our portfolio companies, their biggest challenge would be a tie between product-market fit and hiring. Those are both big topics and huge challenges. Related to hiring, it is amazing how many really smart people with great products and ideas have no idea where to start. Hiring is number one and it is everything. Whether it is trying to hire an engineer or an executive, it's really hard. The biggest challenge of building the company is building the company."

Make no mistake about it: Organizations can reap massive benefits when they find the right talent. In fact, a Boston Consulting Group report noted that being able to deliver on recruiting objectives was the single most important HR capability in terms of economic influence, with the highest competence scoring companies delivering three and a half times revenue growth and two times profit margins relative to the lowest scoring companies.[2] The impact of getting it right is even greater in a startup where individual employees often have a disproportionate impact on firm growth and operate in relatively free-flowing environments without the bureaucratic safeguards of more established firms.[3]

We won't sugarcoat it for you. Planning for and building a solid team is not an easy process for any company, but it can be especially challenging for startups. Employees with the right mix of skills and competencies are expensive and sometimes uninterested in switching firms, which can push startups to the "value bin" of prospects (there are usually legitimate values to be found!). Compounding this issue, prospective employees are typically motivated to project an image of competence and desirability for a job (and may be all too willing to stretch the truth),[4] thereby increasing the likelihood of a "miss." Finally, things can change so quickly in high-growth contexts that your organization's needs are constantly in flux, which can make choosing the right employees feel a lot like guesswork. You absolutely need to have a plan that minimizes errors and reduces painful trade-offs.

The Plan

Successful talent acquisition starts with a workforce plan.[5] A decent workforce plan outlines how many roles are needed, what types of workers are needed, when those workers need to start, and where the workers will be located.

The level of detail varies by organization and stage, but we like to start broadly and work with the financial planning team to ensure budget is in place for both the headcount and the resources required to fill and support a large group of new roles in alignment with the overall business plan discussed with investors and the board. Workforce plans are typically developed in concert with annual company financial planning, both with quarterly check-ins. However, a new capital-raising event in a venture-backed startup is also a critically important time to create a strong workforce plan. Prospective investors will want to know where you intend to spend the new dollars and what organizational capabilities will be enhanced as a result of their capital infusion.

Once you have a reasonable grasp of the basics, you will need to move beyond just a high-level plan. If you intend to hire a large group of new workers—and many organizations double in size with each new funding round—you will want to be very specific about your needs so that the recruiting team, hiring managers, and interview teams can narrow their focus. Stating that you need to hire twenty engineers in San Mateo by the end of the year falls far short of the information needed to effectively source, screen, and select those engineers. What programming languages will they need to know? How experienced will those engineers need to be? How many will do back-end versus front-end engineering, versus IT operations, versus QA? What additional product or engineering management resources will be needed to support that group? What if recruiting is challenging (as it has been for years) and you need to fill a gap? Will you use search firms? Will you pay above market rates? Will you expand the geographic base to include more people? Can some resources be contractors, consultants, or vendors? What needs are the highest priority? Should there be a sequencing to the hiring plan? You get the point. There are many questions to answer before your team can create and execute a quality workforce plan.

Once you understand what the roles that need to be filled look like, you need to decide how you will deliver on those hires. Many early-stage startups rely heavily on personal networks, referrals, and search firms. Those resources are not scalable and present a litany of other problems over time. If you expect to double in size over a year, whether that is twenty new hires or two hundred, you will need to build a legitimate recruitment engine. Even for a startup, that engine should be made up of multiple talent acquisition tools, professionals, and vendors that will help bring you a diverse set of high-quality candidates. You will need to place internal and

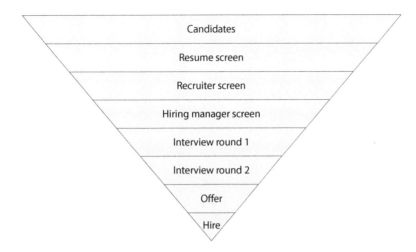

Figure 3.1
Recruitment funnel

recruitment staff and ensure that hiring managers are highly engaged in the process. Once a recruitment engine is in place, multiple parts of that engine should be generating candidates from multiple sources. A strong candidate-sourcing strategy will address inbound active candidates (those proactively reaching out to your company to express interest in positions) and engage passive candidates through outbound contact efforts (such as email campaigns, newsletters, or recruiter phone calls), fully utilizing inexpensive resources to maximize the number of "top of funnel" candidates. Figure 3.1 illustrates this funnel.

The final basic in the talent acquisition arena is to filter candidates, eventually making an offer to those individuals who best meet the needs for your company and its open roles (this is the *selection* process). A good selection process will move interested candidates through a progression of filters that screen out those who are not a fit. Although intuitive at the surface, a practical challenge is developing filters that will both effectively and efficiently (e.g., time, cost) screen candidates while maintaining a positive candidate experience. Interviewing time from hiring managers and their teams is precious, so every hour they spend on the recruitment and hiring process is an hour that they are not writing code, building a better product, or landing new customers. We walk you through some key lessons and tips that will help you navigate the sometimes messy selection waters.

The Basics

Basic 1: Create a workforce plan

A common trap many growing organizations fall into (especially after a substantial funding event) is hastily deploying capital to hire new people, establish new roles, and create entirely new functions without a clear grasp of when those new additions will add value. Even basic workforce planning efforts can greatly increase the effectiveness and efficiency of your organizational build-out. Yet many organizations and individual leaders display a surprisingly strong aversion to the workforce planning process. Our consulting experience suggests the tendency to avoid planning occurs for the same reasons college students often procrastinate on important assignments: tremendous anxiety about the process and not knowing where to start.[6]

Guissu Raafat Baier, cofounder of The People Collective and former vice president of HR at Instacart, says, "Time and time again, I see founders place tremendous focus on modeling business metrics, challenging assumptions, and gathering data when making decisions about product, sales, operations, etc. And yet, when it comes to people and management, that rigor is thrown out the window." Rest assured that workforce planning does not have to be overly complex or reserved only for HR professionals. One way to kick-start your planning efforts is to gather your top leaders around a whiteboard for a few hours to tackle the process outlined in figure 3.2.

You will face a fundamental tension when ramping up for growth: You need to *hire ahead, but not too far ahead.* Our general advice is to keep a twelve- to twenty-four-month time horizon in mind when thinking about how business strategy, customer demand, and your product road map tie into your people plan. Hiring key executives, making significant organizational structure changes, or even bringing a group of frontline marketing employees on board without thinking ahead about the skills, knowledge, and abilities required can result in a complete redo, which is extremely expensive in time, effort, and credibility.

A key tenet of proper headcount expansion is to first estimate the future scope and scale of the most critical teams in your organization. That is, if you have five sales team members today operating with an annual budget of $5 million, you should determine the anticipated team size, structure, and total budget a year from now before hiring begins. Although there will be some degree of uncertainty in these projections, you probably will have

Clarify business needs over next 12–24 months	Make leverage assumptions	Draw org chart for ideal future state organization	Determine transition strategy from current to future state	Identify resource gaps between current and future state
• What promises were made in board decks or investor pitches? • Estimate "widgets" that may impact headcount (customer count, engineering hours, etc.). • Set burn rate and overhead cost constraints.	• Average number of direct reports for each manager (5–15) depending on complexity. • Estimate number of "widgets" per individual contributor (accounts per salesperson, hours per engineer). This is an informal time and motion study.	• No names or specific titles, only boxes, roles, and count. • This is a good time to discuss what work can and should be outsourced. • Run a few different scenarios to see what makes the most sense.	• Think through sequencing and number of steps. • May involve impacts to the existing team (layer, displace, etc.)—determine likely individual outcomes in the future state.	• Revisit preliminary insource versus outsource decisions, including temps, contractors, agencies, and consultants. • Develop your talent acquisition strategy.

Figure 3.2
Workforce planning template

already done a lot of the homework needed to get in the right ballpark. For instance, the "most likely scenario" discussed in your investor pitch deck or board meeting presentations related to the pace of revenue and expense growth are excellent resources. Even if you miss the mark, this estimation exercise should push you toward a smarter headcount expansion.

Be mindful that the purpose of workforce planning is simply to end up with a directional outline of your talent needs. Using your business plan as a foundation, try to formulate your best guess estimates of how many individual contributors are required to produce the number of "widgets" needed in each of your larger functions. In the smaller, more subjective areas (i.e., where no clearly defined "widgets" are produced), ask yourself, "Does this require a full-time job, several jobs, or some fraction of a job?" As you go through your planning, identify each major functional area and assume you will need an expert leader atop each one. As you work through this analysis, think about how expert external resources can be leveraged. A rule of thumb is that if you cannot completely fill up one full-time dedicated role in a function that requires specialized skills or expertise, you are better off outsourcing expertise in that area. Even if this process feels foreign and you lack confidence, do not let yourself get stuck in analysis paralysis. Your assumptions will not be perfect, but they will be much more helpful than having no plan at all.

There are several reasons to avoid overly ambitious or premature hiring efforts. Primary among these reasons is that recruiting, onboarding, and organizing new team members comes with significant expense and distraction. Onboarding new employees is already a risky and stressful endeavor (a substantive number of newcomers usually leave in the first few months after hire), but the outcomes are particularly poor when organizations cannot devote the necessary resources toward their socialization into the organization.[7] As you think about bringing on new employees, consider the following questions: Do you have the capacity to onboard relatively large numbers of new employees? What will a large group of new hires with minimal direction do to your organization? Would contractors, consultants, or third-party providers be able to complete tasks as well as new hires? Finally, how likely is it that a newly recruited senior functional leader will be successful if she does not have clear guidance from senior executives? If you cannot confidently answer these questions, take a step back: You are probably on the path to adding complexity and costs, not actual value.

We concede that there is often an undeniable need to manage investor perception by deploying capital rapidly, so some near-immediate hiring momentum is inevitable. The most successful leaders, however, are those who avoid spending excessively on headcount when they are unsure exactly how they will utilize the new employees. They do not, for instance, build a large sales team after their Series A investment if the company has not yet found clear product-market fit and does not have customer onboarding capabilities in place. Rather, they are constantly aware of the stage of maturation of their company and willing to work their growth plan methodically from one stage to the next.

Basic 2: Define the roles you want to fill

Your workforce planning effort should identify the roles you need to fill. However, before your team can fill those roles, or even develop a strategy to fill those roles, a lot more information should be collected. Primarily, this means articulating the tasks, duties, and responsibilities (TDRs) of each role as well as the knowledge, skills, abilities, and other characteristics (KSAOs) an employee will need to fulfill the role. Although seemingly tedious to first-time planners, do not shirk on this part of the process. Indeed, job analysis is in many ways the most fundamental building block in an HR system because it influences nearly every other aspect of the people management function (e.g., recruiting, selection, compensation, training, and performance management).[8] To that end, the work you invest in this stage will pay dividends later.

If you have a skilled department head or hiring manager in place, this person should be able to generally articulate the TDRs and KSAOs for roles on their team. If you need more detail, ask current employees in similar roles for their insight or borrow from other organizations' postings. The federal government maintains a free database of job titles and details (Occupational Network, or "O*Net") that can serve as a useful starting point for many types of roles your organization may need to fill, and most compensation benchmarking reports offer brief descriptions of hundreds of the most common roles. Finally, the Society for Human Resource Management (SHRM) also maintains several tools and templates you can use to build out a reasonable job analysis. The point is that you do not need to re-create the wheel. Much like the workforce plan, you need not worry about getting the process exactly right (things will inevitably change anyway). Focus on trying to give your organization reasonable goalposts before recruiting begins. We provide sample role descriptions in the following list.

SAMPLE ROLE DESCRIPTIONS

ROLE: VP MARKETING

Immediate Manager: CEO
Top executive responsible for overseeing the overall marketing function. Responsibilities include overseeing product marketing, assessment of existing and potential markets, evaluation of pricing strategies, marketing communications, channel marketing, performance marketing, brand management, public relations, user engagement, and contract administration. Responsible for developing long-range marketing plans for the company and translating the overall strategy into tactical plans to achieve the company's goals and objectives.

- Leads a team with multiple management layers.
- Typically possesses an advanced degree in a related field.
- Typically possesses fifteen-plus years of relevant experience.

ROLE: SOFTWARE ENGINEER 4

Immediate Manager: Manager, Engineering
Plans, designs, develops, and tests software systems or applications for software enhancements and new products including cloud-based or internet-related tools. Advanced knowledge of Python, Java, and ReactJS required.

- Typically an individual contributor.
- Typically possesses a bachelor's degree in a related field.
- Typically possesses seven-plus years of relevant experience.

Not all positions need to be filled by full-time employees. In fact, some roles may best be filled by temporary workers, contractors, vendors, consultants, or advisors. These types of nonpermanent "contingent workers" can provide invaluable support and cover for vacancies in particularly hard-to-fill or urgently needed positions. They can also provide short-term support while your organization figures out exactly what it will need for the next twelve to twenty-four months. Startups are awash in ambiguity, so it is easy to be tripped up by a number of decision-making fallacies (e.g., analysis paralysis or hasty hiring). Contingent hires can serve as a

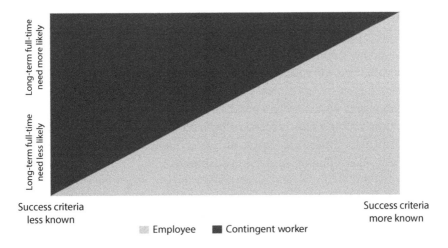

Figure 3.3
Staffing decision analysis

nice compromise or bridge while leaders take time to test and refine their plans. Figure 3.3 provides a simple illustration of the tension between the certainty of a "long-term need" (twelve to twenty-four months) and clarity of the success criteria for the role (TDRs and KSAOs).

As needs become more well defined, they should also be prioritized. Most startup leaders understand that it is important for your organization to hire engineers to build the product before you hire salespeople to sell it. Often overlooked, however, is the importance of hiring senior leaders before hiring their teams (to the extent possible). When a new leader is brought into the organization, that person is often expected to make a rapid impact to meet certain expected results (which were specified if you effectively defined the role during the hiring process). However, expectations of making a *rapid* impact are often impeded when a new leader is forced to retain existing team members the leader would not have selected if given a choice.[9]

Consider the following example. A new chief technology officer (CTO) wants to implement an Agile Kanban software development approach, but the existing team is experienced only in Agile Scrum. Perhaps that same CTO decides it is most effective to outsource a significant part of the infrastructure team with a vendor, but she is then forced to redeploy talent into areas with which they are unfamiliar. Maybe there is a work style difference between the new leader and some of the previously hired employees, or the new leader has a few people she knows well that she wants to bring onboard. In all these cases, a lot of work is involved in redeploying or rebuilding the team—possibly more work than building from a "green field" environment. If you think you will soon bring in a new senior leader for a group, fill only the most urgent roles on that team until that new leader is in place, and use contingent workers where possible. The search for people who will lead large teams should take precedence in recruitment efforts. The larger the department, and the more layers of management, the higher the priority typically is for filling the leadership positions.

Basic 3: Build a candidate generation engine

Once you have a workforce plan in place, a good idea of what each role will look like, and leadership roles prioritized at the top of the list, your next challenge is finding workers who can help you carry out your business plans. To maximize chances for success, expand the size of your candidate pool by taking full advantage of the most common low-cost online resources for job seekers and by leveraging the power of your employee network through referral applicants before expanding into other sourcing channels. If you've hired more than a handful of people, you already know that not all recruiting sources are created equal. As you consider new sourcing channels, be mindful of whether they give you access to a broad, diverse set of talent (your referral engine will likely amplify "same as me" tendencies, so new channels are an important complement).

Figure 3.4 provides preliminary guidance for evaluating recruiting sources. Notice that there is not a check in every box. Indeed, you must learn to "fish where the fish are" if you want to acquire the right talent quickly and within budget. Time and money can be quickly sucked into inefficient candidate generation activities that are rarely productive enough to merit consideration for a business that is attempting to scale rapidly. Unless there is a unique business reason, you can generally avoid job fairs, meetups, conferences, and networking lunches while your business is scaling. Focus and efficiency are paramount for startups.[10]

Different needs will be best served through different sourcing strategies, so put some attention into several of these channels. Employment branding and job postings on the major sites will suit nearly every type of need, and it does not take a lot of investment to get these basics into place. Any growing company with more than twenty employees should consider

	First Dozen Hires	Head of Department	Niche, Specialized Roles	Most Professional Roles	Entry Level Roles
Employment branding (internal career site, Glassdoor, LinkedIn, Indeed employer pages)		X	X	X	X
Paid job postings on major sites (Indeed, LinkedIn, Monster, Facebook, etc.)		X	X	X	X
Paid job postings on niche sites (Mediabistro, Dice, Upwork, Handshake, etc.)			X		
Online resume and profile search		X	X	X	
Contract- or temp-to-hire		X	X	X	X
Phone networking		X	X		
Executive search firm		X	X		
Personal networks	X				
In-person networking (Meetups, conferences)	X				

Figure 3.4
Talent sourcing diagnostic

Table 3.1
Candidate sourcing strategies

---

1. Ensure that your company website has robust "About Us" and "Careers" sections, with jobs posted and online applications supported.

2. Complete at least a basic company profile on major employment sites (Indeed, LinkedIn, Glassdoor).

3. Provide a high level of clarity regarding any roles you are trying to fill: what it does, where it can reside, what experience/career level it will be, how it will fit into the organization.

4. Price the job using a high-quality market data source for benchmarking purposes. Establish a total cash compensation range from the 25th to the 75th percentile of the market.

5. Write a simple, clear, and compelling job posting that attracts candidates. Post internally and to all major job boards.

6. Drive internal referrals by ensuring that existing employees are aware of the opening and the targeted candidate profile. Referral bonuses are unnecessary; publicity is more valuable than incentives.

7. Source passive candidates by reviewing profiles on LinkedIn, contacting prospects who might be a match for the target candidate profile, and asking those individuals for referrals.

---

investing in a membership in Glassdoor, adding a careers section to their public website, and completing their company profile page on LinkedIn and Indeed. Set aside a portion of your recruitment budget for postings on the major job boards (e.g., Indeed, Monster, and Glassdoor), and provide access to a LinkedIn Recruiter account subscription. The largest recruitment expenses will generally be comprised of internal recruiter headcount, agency search fees, temp-to-hire conversion fees, and recruitment tools. We suggest that recruitment tools be your first investment, accounting for about 20 percent of your total recruitment budget. Employment branding services, high-quality job postings, thoughtfully configured applicant tracking systems, and resume search subscription services can dramatically enhance recruitment effectiveness across all sourcing channels. Our suggested strategies are summarized in table 3.1.

Basic 4: Construct a recruitment team

Even with a strong employment brand, good postings, a clear employee value proposition (i.e., the "What's in it for me?" [WIIFM] of working for your company), and engaged hiring managers, you will need dedicated internal *and* external recruitment support as hiring volume increases.

Your well of referrals will eventually run dry, and you don't want to spend too much capital on search fees.

The basis of any good recruitment team is the hiring manager. Ensure that your hiring managers are fully engaged in recruitment activities and view themselves as ultimately responsible for ensuring that the job is filled quickly with a good candidate. Share the candidate WIIFM with managers and have them practice sharing that "sell story" until they are able to comfortably articulate a compelling message with prospects. Set the top-down expectation that each manager working to fill a role on a team should be dedicating three to five hours per week per opening. Otherwise candidates are likely to go stale, and recruiters will waste time chasing feedback.

Hiring manager involvement starts with a high-quality "intake meeting" with a recruiter, co-creating a candidate scorecard for the role, sharing where candidates can most likely be found, determining who will participate in the selection process (i.e., on an interview panel) and how feedback and follow-up will work. Table 3.2 provides an intake meeting checklist. A thoughtful intake meeting accelerates all other activities downstream. In addition to an intake meeting, hiring managers should be expected to screen resumes (to help the recruiter home in on target candidates) and complete brief video/phone screens (prior to onsite interviews). Depending on the stage of a search, hiring managers may also be reaching out to their personal network, posting on social media, conducting reference checks, or preparing an onboarding plan. Hiring is an enormous time investment for hiring managers[11] and cannot easily be offloaded to others in the organization. In startups, even the best recruiters will struggle to cover for an absentee hiring manager, and their efforts to do so usually result in an unnecessarily long and frustrating process for everyone involved.

Hiring managers need to be involved in startup hiring, but recruiters and search firms can play vital support roles. They charge hefty fees, to be

Table 3.2
Hiring manager intake meeting checklist

1. Job scorecard developed (five to fifteen criteria that candidates can be compared against).
2. Sourcing strategy identified (where candidates are likely to be found—schools, companies, groups, etc.).
3. Selection process outlined (sequencing of interviews, total number of steps, who is on the team, etc.).
4. Hiring manager responsibilities reviewed (response time for feedback, onboarding plan, etc.).

sure, but a good executive search firm will have a highly skilled team of professionals. In many cases, these firms specialize in a functional area, industry, or geography. Search firms are best used to fill high-priority roles (i.e., senior leader) that are in particularly high demand in your market. Exhaust viable leads from your network and other recruiting channels before hiring a search firm. At the time of this writing, many top search firms are oversubscribed and turn down more searches than they accept, so you will have to work to find a valuable partner. We recommend talking to your venture capital talent partner or a trusted advisor to identify a short list of firms (and, more important, the lead search partner) who can best meet your needs. The best search firms have deep networks of existing relationships in their vertical(s) and can often get potential candidates interested who may otherwise never have known about or considered the role (research suggests that "passive" hiring is an increasingly important and viable strategy).[12] A search fee is typically 20 to 35 percent of the annual base pay per placement, paid out over three installments. Although some firms may take searches on a contingent basis (i.e., paid only if they make the placement), the top firms tend to work on retainer only (receiving a portion at the start of the search, another portion at presentation of candidates, and the final payment after the new hire starts work).

Executive search firms add substantial value by corralling overwhelmed leadership teams and educating founders about talent markets and functions in which they lack expertise, but they are not the best option for every job that needs to be filled. Compared to the high rates that search firms charge, an internal recruiter finding as few as five to seven professional hires per year may be cost-effective. However, half a dozen hires in a year rarely justifies a full-time job, thereby presenting a challenge for startups caught on the fence. We suggest starting out by consolidating internal recruitment and new hire activities (posting jobs, scheduling interviews, collecting feedback, completing new hire paperwork, onboarding administration, etc.) under an office manager or an executive assistant until your company is hiring ten to twenty people per year. At that point, you should hire your first HR professional who can take the lead in both of these areas. When your company needs to hire twenty or more nonexecutive positions in a year, it is probably time to invest in a full-time professional recruiter.

As your hiring needs grow, so too will your recruitment team, and more formalized processes will be necessary to manage the increasing volume. Most startups struggle to create sufficient talent acquisition capacity, so we often recommend considering recruitment process outsourcing (RPO) solutions to supplement internal recruitment teams, recruiting contractors, and search firm arrangements. An RPO can also provide almost instant infrastructure, accelerating the maturity of your recruitment function by leveraging the experience of people who have built many functions at many companies. As the talent acquisition function grows to ten, twenty, and beyond, be sure to define service level agreements and performance expectations for the recruiting team and start measuring key steps and elements of the recruitment process. Small improvements at scale can yield big results.

Basic 5: Use effective selection processes

For an organization to grow quickly while maintaining (or raising) the bar on quality of hire, it needs to construct a rational selection process, invest in the right tools (there are a lot of bad ones), rely on data as much as possible, and help managers become better hiring managers. Table 3.3 outlines

Table 3.3
Candidate selection and assessment approach

Recommended Approach	Candidate Pass-Through Rate
1. Recruiter and hiring manager co-create a job scorecard outlining the ten to twenty elements that define the ideal candidate on paper.	n/a
2. Initial candidate profile is reviewed by recruiter.	<10%
3. Follow-up candidate profile is reviewed by hiring manager (ensures recruiter is in alignment with hiring manager's expectations).	>20%
4. Phone/video screen by recruiter (about fifteen minutes) to check interest and alignment with role expectations, location, and compensation. If not a fit, ask the candidate for referrals.	~50%
5. Phone/video screen by hiring manager (about thirty minutes).	~50%
6. First onsite interview by hiring manager (about ninety minutes), using a structured interview format—consider asking for work product examples at this time.	~66%
7. Second onsite interview by interview panel consisting of manager of hiring manager, peers, and key internal partners (maximum of five separate interviews of about forty-five minutes each).	~66%
8. Background check initiated by recruitment team.	~95%
9. Reference checks by hiring manager.	<90%
10. Offer made.	>90%

a candidate selection and assessment approach that can serve as a template for most professional roles within growing companies.

"Pass-through rates" refer to the percentage of candidates who proceed in the process following that step. If too many or not enough candidates are falling out, the process is not working properly. Each step of the selection process should reduce time by everyone else later in the process without unduly restricting the candidate pipeline (in other words, avoid eliminating candidates who would otherwise be successful). It is critical for the recruiter, the hiring manager, and talent acquisition leadership to be in close contact when something goes awry. Missteps can usually be traced to an information gap or misalignment of expectations, which can be quickly rectified with early intervention.

During the selection process, it is important to maintain a positive candidate experience to optimize the efficiency of the selection funnel. To this end, research clearly suggests that applicants who hold a favorable view of the selection process are more likely to accept an offer.[13] Candidates that are not a fit should be dismissed professionally, politely, and promptly as early in the process as possible. As a startup, your reputation matters, and word of mouth about inefficient or awkward selection processes travels fast. Moreover, keeping unqualified applicants in your funnel for too long absorbs significant time by the hiring manager and the recruiter working the role.

Research suggests that a rigorous and fair selection process tends to improve applicant reactions and reduces chances of litigation.[14] That said, do not overcomplicate the selection process. We have worked with clients who have had six-plus onsite interview rounds, twelve-plus interviewers on a panel, and multiple skills and personality assessments applied throughout the process. Excessive interviews, especially unstructured, free-flowing types, can be problematic. As Wharton Professor Peter Cappelli writes, "Just winging it and asking whatever comes to mind is next to useless. More important, interviews are where biases most easily show up."[15] Less can be more. In a growing company, time is in short supply and is a priceless, nonrenewable resource. Although the process discussed here won't be the perfect fit for every role, it can serve as a good starting point.

We cannot summarize the mountains of research on selection assessments in such a condensed space, but we do want to acknowledge that management and industrial-organizational (I-O) psychology researchers have spent the better part of a century evaluating the validity of various selection techniques (and you do not need to be an I-O PhD to use Google Scholar).

However, we want to caution you to be wary of the myriad "bad" (i.e., invalid) assessment tools being marketed and the prevalence of using "good" tools in the wrong way. Speaking to this point, Brian Swider, a prominent HR professor (University of Florida), told us, "HR consultants are often selling the same sort of intuitively appealing, but scientifically unfounded selection systems that companies were already using before deciding they should seek the help of 'experts' to identify the best people for a job. But I have never heard of consulting firms giving refunds when their products don't deliver on the initial promises."

A few foundational activities will help you identify the appropriate process and tools. First, obtain a clear understanding of the role and ensure that anyone participating on an interview panel has a similarly well-rounded perspective. If the job already exists within your organization, create a "success profile" that outlines the key skills and abilities of a successful incumbent. It is better to select first on skills and abilities rather than relying on ambiguous and potentially harmful "fit" assessments during the selection process. If the job does not currently exist within your organization, the hiring manager and recruiter can create a draft of a success profile together using good judgment and the closest relevant internal comparison to construct a model.

Avoid overly broad personality or style tests that are grounded in unproven pseudo-science; they are often unreliable and irrelevant for your jobs. Examples of frequently misused tests include Emergenetics, DiSC, Personality Indicator (PI), and the Myers-Briggs Type Indicator (MBTI).[16] If you are convinced that you need a personality test, consider starting with the International Personality Item Pool,[17] which has numerous public domain (i.e., free) survey items that have been validated in hundreds of research studies.[18] Furthermore, before using your newfound assessment tools on prospective applicants, run concurrent validation tests on your current employees. Concurrent validation exercises simply involve administering your prospective assessments (e.g., Big Five Personality Traits, IQ) to current employees, and then exploring the results to identify meaningful relationships between your predictors and actual job performance (the outcome). If you see no relationship between agreeableness and sales success among your current workers, for instance, you probably do not need to make agreeableness a metric of interest in your salesperson selection funnel. Concurrent validations are not a perfect indicator of selection tool success and are mostly constrained to existing job types in your organization, but they can give you some baseline information and help you stay clear of simple mistakes. Where concurrent validations are impossible or not meaningful, keep track of your applicant assessment data, and evaluate its predictive validity with new hire performance every few months. Measurement of both your talent sourcing and selection efforts is key to refining and optimizing your talent acquisition efforts.

A few final words about risks in selection processes. Many companies boast as high as a 50 percent referral rate. That means half of their hires are referred by existing employees. A skilled and trusted team member putting a good word in for someone can be incredibly valuable. It first indicates that the team member is engaged enough to recommend your organization to a friend, and it also brings a certain measure of credibility to the candidate. However, personal networks can be powerful *and* dangerous.[19] Nepotism, favoritism, and other biases can quickly spring up in organizations that rely too much on "the friends and family plan." A company's culture toward diversity and inclusion, in particular, is significantly shaped by talent acquisition efforts and how underrepresented people are treated upon joining.[20] Being mindful of your company's prospective composition early on can significantly improve the efficacy of later DEI initiatives and help mitigate even more serious, and harder to fix, issues later. In summary, we generally agree with the premise that good people know other good people, but this is hardly justification for skipping a thoughtful candidate selection and assessment process.

The same point holds true for temp-to-hire and contract-to-hire conversions. To be sure, contingent arrangements are a great way to get to know a prospective employee prior to a full commitment, but there is an innate danger in the convenience of that conversion. Hiring managers are under tremendous pressure to get their own work done while filling the jobs on their team. They will, inevitably, be tempted to convert someone to meet an immediate need simply because it is the easiest option even though that person might not be the best long-term fit. Help your managers preserve the bandwidth they need to do a great job building the team.

Conclusion

Many startups have inexperienced hiring managers who do not know what a complete planning and talent acquisition process should look like. Your talent acquisition team, whether that is a formal or informal designation, must take a leadership role in educating them. To that end, invest heavily in helping managers become better hiring managers. Acknowledge that they will need bandwidth to do a great job, and give them the tools, training, and evidence to succeed. If your organization does not yet have a recruitment leader who can do this, engage an RPO or an outside advisor to help you construct and strengthen your strategy and approach. Their experienced support can help you identify the best methods for your organization and avoid unintended consequences such as bias or discrimination creeping into the process. And, as always, measure your successes and failures so you can adjust toward more optimal approaches as you grow.

4

Total Rewards

Creating a Compelling Employment Value Proposition

Assembling the best possible employee team is near the top of the list when it comes to the most challenging issues startup entrepreneurs encounter as they look to scale their organizations. With employee compensation and unemployment rates at record highs, attracting and retaining the right employee team is critical to an organization's growth and, if not approached properly, can stall the entire company. Additionally, the world of human resources has become increasingly complex with the emergence of legal rules pertaining to gig-economy workers, sick-leave administration, FMLA, etc., as well as with competition-mandated employee benefits like robust health insurance packages, retirement programs, high-deductible accounts, well-being programs, and other flashy employee offerings. Early stage entrepreneurs who attempt to solve for these challenges directly by assigning headcount to HR, establishing and managing multiple vendor relationships, and standing up an internal function often quickly find themselves in a counterintuitive situation: Their employee benefits program is weaker, they are noncompliant in more areas, and they are spending more money than they would have if they had simply outsourced this work.

—JESSE FREESE, SENIOR BUSINESS CONSULTANT AT
SEQUOIA AND FOUNDER OF STARTUP EXPERTS

Early on, it's about getting past the idea stage and finding product-market fit. From a talent lens, success is all about recruiting. HR is nowhere in the picture, and the emphasis is on speed and flexibility. But fast forward toward one hundred employees and the focus changes dramatically. From the time when everyone knew everyone and operated in the same small digs in SoMa, now the workforce is distributed, sizable, and diverse in tenure, ability, and impact. The talent focus shifts from "butts in seats" to "how do I motivate and retain the talent I now have?"

Employers ideally would shift focus proactively, but often it is reactive. Employees start demanding to know about their career path, opportunities for more pay, and clarity on how their performance stacks up relative to others. At this stage, putting in place a foundation for rewards and a philosophy is critical. Just as you have business planning to determine how to invest your capital and track results, the same idea exists in how you generate value from your greatest asset—your talent. So it's imperative to understand how you are rewarding employees today, what you are rewarding them for, and how you want to reward them in the future. In short, you need a total rewards philosophy to be a "north star" for directing rewards to the right people for the right reason. And to make it even more challenging, that philosophy needs to be consistent yet flexible and fair across the employees you have and the next few hundred you're about to hire.

—ASHISH RAINA, FOUNDER OF OPTIMIZE TALENT,
FORMER HEAD OF COMPENSATION AT BOX, AND TALENT
PARTNER AT INDEX VENTURES

CHAPTER 4 RUNDOWN

The Problem
How do you attract workers without burning through cash and equity too quickly?

The Plan
Put together a minimum viable total rewards package, then identify a realistic employee value proposition you can deliver.

The Basics
1. Offer competitive cash compensation.
2. Offer strong core benefits.
3. Be selective about additional perks and programs.
4. Create an equity ownership plan.
5. Clarify the employment value proposition.

The Problem

No matter how much time and effort you spend designing a talent acquisition strategy, its success will be inextricably linked to the value proposition perceived by prospective hires, referred to as the "employment value proposition" (EVP). In other words, if you are asking candidates to give up their time, talent, energy, and other opportunities to benefit your organization, the return had better be worth it. Research by Gartner indicates that companies "can reduce the compensation premium by 50 percent and reach 50 percent deeper into the labor market when candidates view an EVP as attractive" and "decrease annual employee turnover by just under 70 percent and increase new hire commitment by nearly 30 percent."[1] Competition levels can vary across some functional specialties and geographical areas (e.g., software engineers in San Francisco versus call center staff in Jacksonville), although constructing and communicating an EVP that is compatible with the relevant labor market is paramount in all cases.

Your company's story, a leader's charisma, and many other intangibles can move the needle for prospective talent. But these alone are rarely enough to effectively attract and retain talent in a competitive environment. To give your company an advantage, you must get a handle on the "total rewards" package (a broad term we use to capture the mix of pay, benefits, perks, and programs offered to workers) that your targeted workers *need* and *most strongly want*. Understanding your targeted workers' priorities is critical for avoiding prohibitively expensive, if not outright impossible, "do it all" approaches. Equally problematic are the random patchwork offerings that emerge from too much "best practice implementation" and not enough critical thinking.

The scale and speed of the talent arms race, especially in popular venture-backed startup communities, has caused a troubling number of employers to implement costly programs and practices that deliver negligible value (we're looking at you, ping-pong tables and free food).[2] The prevalence of these low-value offerings is so high that they are influencing best practice benchmarking in the startup community—the "all the cool kids are doing it" effect. Unfortunately, many well-intentioned but less experienced people leaders end up encouraging their organizations to become early adopters of seemingly innovative programs, practices, and technologies that, at best, fail to meaningfully influence their EVP and, at worst, cause their organization to run aground under the weight of the administrative complexity and attention dispersion accompanied by a plethora of programs. Trying to keep up with the Joneses by copying and pasting the practices and programs of well-known organizations is extremely dangerous and can quickly derail your organization.

The Plan

Founders often ask us, "When should we start thinking about pay, benefits, equity plans, and employee programs?" Our response: "Right away!" Even with your original founding team you should construct a minimum viable total rewards offering (i.e., the table stakes you need to play the talent game). A minimum viable offering is simply one that does not actively scare off large groups of workers from joining and staying at your organization (this typically occurs if you leave out a program that workers view as essential).

After you have established a minimum viable total rewards offering, invest in effective administration and compelling communication of your core programs. Emphasizing clarity and maximizing the appeal of what you can offer is critical. A minimal viable offering may vary by industry, geography, and current labor markets, but the core for most high-growth companies is *competitive base pay, health benefits*, and *an equity plan*. You will have a hard time attracting *any* workers at a startup without these core programs.

Once the foundation is established, you can explore ways to enhance your EVP with more targeted plans, programs, and other nuanced benefits. To avoid costly errors, focus on selecting only a few programs that are particularly meaningful to your target worker population and invest in making those programs outstanding. You must have the bandwidth and focus to consistently administer programs for a positive employee experience and compellingly communicate the benefit to maximize worker commitment and alignment to the company mission. If you cannot ensure consistent administration and compelling communication of existing programs, you should probably think twice before adding a new program. Do not think in terms of whether any individual program or practice is "good" or "bad," but instead consider how it might affect your organization in its current context. Good leaders will not choose between offering "best practice" programs and running an effective business; they will ruthlessly prioritize and selectively implement programs that attract and retain the type of workers they need to be successful.

The Basics

Basic 1: Offer competitive cash compensation

Beyond the initial group of founders (who usually have higher equity stakes), you are almost certainly going to need to offer competitive cash compensation (primarily base pay) to attract and retain workers. A 2019 report by Mercer (a consulting and advisory firm that collects mountains of employee survey data) suggests that compensation is the foundation of a successful EVP.[3] Although this can feel daunting as a startup, remember that base pay is just one aspect of the EVP—a critical aspect, no doubt, but not the only aspect. Startups can sometimes be successful in trading a portion of "typical" base pay (e.g., salary) for other benefits such as equity or experiential elements (e.g., unique professional growth opportunities, association with a hot brand, or the opportunity to work with a new technology).

In practice, the compensation discount a startup can reasonably offer diminishes rapidly once a startup becomes more mature. Although every startup is somewhat unique, our rule of thumb is that compensation discounts become especially problematic when an organization reaches one hundred employees and raises significant capital, usually after a Series C investment. At that stage, workers will expect their pay to be "trued up" to market rates. In addition, early employees are likely to be deep into their equity vesting period, meaning that the equity is a less effective retention device (the golden handcuffs are loosening). Although the theoretical value of the organization is probably increasing, the risk of attrition is high if you do not get these pay decisions right.[4]

A simple but surprisingly difficult question to answer when thinking about competitive compensation is "*What is the market rate?*" Across similar jobs, the size of an organization as measured by employee count and gross revenue is still typically the most important factor associated with total compensation, far more important than geography, industry, and other factors. However, as a startup planning for rapid growth, you may very well be competing for talent with other startups as well as with giant companies (e.g., Facebook, Amazon, Netflix, Google, Microsoft, and Salesforce) that have reliable revenue and relatively predictable operations. In that case, using company size as a baseline comparison anchor may not be particularly useful.

The giants (usually publicly traded) are typically positioned to offer better base pay and fringe benefits to their employees than are smaller companies. They also may offer equity to many workers, usually in the form of Restricted Stock Units (RSUs), and the value of that equity tends to be more predictable and similar to cash. The pay mix at smaller growth companies is normally weighted somewhat lighter on cash and fringes and heavier on equity. The obvious advantage for high-growth startups is the upside of their equity. If your organization has a strong growth story and is paired with a reasonable likelihood of a liquidity event, you can effectively compete with the behemoths and their deep pocketbooks by adjusting the compensation mix. Communicating the potential value of your company's equity grants can be tricky (and a warning: the lawyers *hate* it), but doing so is absolutely vital if you hope to compete for talent while offering any discount to the current cash value of your compensation package.

The best way to determine market rates for your organization's jobs is to get a good benchmarking survey report early. Your prospective and current employees are probably researching pay rates on free sites such as Salary.com, Glassdoor.com, AngelList, and WealthFront. These sites can offer some modestly helpful guidance to an employer, but we typically recommend investing a few thousand dollars in a more targeted compensation survey from one of the major consulting firms in your industry. For U.S.-based technology startups, two high-quality data providers currently are Option Impact by Advanced HR and Radford (an Aon company). If you are lucky enough to be funded by a major VC firm (such as Sequoia, NEA, IVP, or A16Z), your talent partner will probably have a portfolio company compensation survey to share with you for free.

The benefit of using a high-quality compensation survey is the accuracy of the data. Reputable compensation surveys are completed by professionals under strict guidelines and controls, very much in contrast to the "anyone can enter anything" methodology behind most free, publicly available sources. Alas, finding quality benchmarking data and using it wisely are two different animals. Given the subtle nuance between companies and the ever-changing talent environment, no data will be perfectly precise. Thus you must view the available data as an approximation and allow it to guide (versus dictate) good, logical judgment.

To help in this process, we recommend that organizations establish targeted compensation ranges for their jobs *in advance of recruiting for the role*. Thoughtfully establishing those ranges before reaching the offer stage with a candidate provides excellent screening criteria (i.e., "this person is more junior/senior than what we're looking for") and establishes bounds of reasonability when competition arises. Setting ranges also helps to mute unintended pay variations within a team, which can lead to a number of serious (and surprisingly long-lasting) cultural, ethical, legal, and performance-related dangers.[5] Ranges should be used as guidance for good judgment rather than as a hard floor or ceiling.

In the absence of a planned and disciplined approach to pay ranges, even the best-intentioned organizations will fall prey to avoidable traps. In competitive labor markets, wages can be rapidly driven up by organizations competing on limited information. One particularly common pitfall is relying too strongly on anecdotal market information from candidates themselves. When a qualified candidate claims to be making a premium above your organization's range at their current job or has a higher offer elsewhere, that information may very well be useful, real-time market intelligence worth considering . . . or not. Research clearly suggests that candidates are motivated to place themselves in a self-benefiting light that, in some cases, translates into half-truths or outright fabrications manifesting in their job searches.[6] Just because Candidate A claims to be making a certain amount does not mean that is the right number for your organization.

Be wary also that you and your organization's hiring managers, no matter how professional, are human beings capable of bias and irrational decision-making.[7] When a hiring manager likes a candidate who wants more salary than your range allows, it is very easy for the manager to build a compelling, seemingly rational case for why a deviance should be allowed. Similarly, hiring managers and recruiters are both incented to fill jobs with the highest-caliber candidate quickly, but usually without direct regard to the cost of that worker. If you tend to outbid your competitors for talent, you will not necessarily have the best workers—just the *best paid* workers. Indeed, research suggests that organizations are particularly susceptible to overpaying when evaluating external talent,[8] so vigilance is key.

How should you balance sticking to your predetermined rate with making an exception? When presented with anecdotal information questioning your salary range, actively look for broader patterns that might disconfirm or support whether this information should be used to alter your approach. Ask questions like these: Are current employees in similar roles and similar pay actively seeking other jobs? Are most of our prospective employees for a particular role balking at our offer, or just a few? What sort of situation is this candidate coming from? What are her or his alternatives? Placing some bumpers around your recruiting team and hiring managers can be especially helpful in mitigating unnecessary compensation bloat.

In the context of the overall EVP, understanding how your company's compensation stacks up in the market can save millions of salary dollars, meaningful runway time, and all sorts of internal pay equity issues. We have provided you with enough information to get started and to keep you away from the most common traps, but we would be remiss not to acknowledge that compensation is a complicated topic with entire textbooks devoted to its theory and practice.[9] Consequently, engaging a seasoned compensation professional to help you determine an appropriate *compensation philosophy* for your organization is incredibly valuable. A compensation philosophy will help you to determine who your competitors for talent are (which may vary by job type); which survey(s) you will use for benchmarking purposes; how you want to be positioned versus your competitors (i.e., tend to be the 50th percentile for most jobs but 60th percentile for specific roles); what ranges you will share with candidates, hiring managers, and recruiters; what the internal career path at your organization will be; and what controls and norms you will want to establish related to hires, promotions, and pay changes.

Basic 2: Offer strong core benefits

Today the most essential nonsalary offering is health insurance.[10] Without health insurance, many nonfounder employees will balk at the prospect of working for your organization, thereby severely limiting your talent acquisition efforts. Despite popular opinion from inexperienced leaders, health insurance is relatively simple and not overly costly relative to the potential return in attracting/retaining talent. It also can be easily supplemented with other insurance add-ons—dental, life, long- and short-term disability, and long-term care—which provides some latitude in deciding how extensive you want your offering to be.

The simplest way to set up a suitable health care plan is to find a benefits broker and select a strong basic medical offering.[11] Most medical benefits programs adopt a variation of two basic cost-sharing designs: 100 percent monthly premium of an employee, with 50–80 percent of their dependent premiums covered by the employer; or 70–80 percent of total monthly premium costs covered by the employer (regardless of the number of employee dependents). Recent total cost estimates for health benefits (including both employer and employee spend) are around $7,000 for single coverage and $20,000 for family coverage.[12] Of course, employee and employer costs vary widely based on broker fees, plan design, the cost-share design, and the number of dependents. We encourage companies to shift to a flat fee structure quickly to provide cost transparency.

Benefits and related brokerage expenses are often embedded in the structure of a professional employer organization (PEO), which can be an excellent solution for most early-stage startups. Under a PEO arrangement, your organization manages employees' daily activities, but the PEO is contractually designated as a co-employer of your workers for administrative purposes, enabling them to seamlessly handle payroll processing, timekeeping, payroll tax filings, benefits (e.g., insurance, vacation), and retirement. Many PEOs also offer compliance and training assistance and human resources information systems (HRIS) technology support. A PEO can be billed on a flat, per employee basis, or as a percentage of payroll. Some estimates suggest that annual per employee fees typically range from $900 to $1,500 whereas percentage-based models typically bill at 3 to 10 percent of payroll.[13] Large, reputable companies in this space include ADP Total Source, Insperity, Justworks, TriNet, Sequoia One, and Paychex.

Aside from providing instant infrastructure for payroll, benefits, compliance, and many other administrative items, one of the greatest advantages of a PEO is access to pooled health insurance coverage at much lower costs than small companies could obtain individually. This works because a PEO can negotiate rates based on a much larger total employee pool, consisting of the aggregate number of employees that it employs on behalf of its clients. With the insurance price savings due to increased purchasing power, the cost of a PEO is almost entirely offset for many organizations, making it an attractive option for many startups.

Even with all the advantages, leaning on a PEO can only take startups so far. PEOs are great for delivering basic services to up to 150+ employees, but they are less appropriate beyond that point. Once a company crosses 100–150 employees, insourcing certain payroll and HR transactional activities is more economically efficient and offers more flexibility and control over data and programs. However, the shift from PEO to insourced support can be complex and potentially disruptive (you are messing with how people are paid!). Thus you need to engage experienced resources during implementation and allocate enough time to get it right. You can anticipate a four- to six-month transition process *after* you have selected the full complement of replacement providers and negotiated their contracts. Also, be mindful of where you are in the calendar year. When rolling off a PEO midyear, employees will likely need to restart their tax withholdings, re-enroll in benefits programs, haggle with complexities in their flex spending accounts, and ultimately receive multiple W-2s. The organization will also wrestle with complicated payroll accounting issues and implementation support demands in the accounting, finance, and IT departments. Accordingly, we recommend that companies schedule a PEO transition at the end of the year or quarter to minimize some of these challenges.

Whenever you choose to leave a PEO—assuming you are fortunate enough to grow to the size that it makes sense—be prepared to provide your own solutions for payroll, payroll taxes, benefits administration, workers compensation, employment practices liability insurance (EPLI), retirement plans, employment counsel, and the many other services PEOs provide. It can be an imposing transition, which results in a lot of organizations continuing with their PEO longer than they would prefer. All that said, a PEO is an excellent solution for most startups. Just be sure to plan ahead and select a provider that can scale with you for at least a few years.

Basic 3: Selectively offer a few perks and programs that support your EVP

A multitude of perks, benefits, and programs can bolster your company's employment value proposition (EVP). Focus on what matters most, and be wary of vendors pitching outlandish returns on investment (ROIs) on fringe benefit offerings.

Startups should be mindful of the trade-offs involved in implementing any new employee program, especially as they move away from the standard benefit categories (e.g., health insurance) toward trendier offerings (e.g., free dog walking). Expenses, both direct and indirect, increase rapidly as you scale. A $1,000 individual technology allowance, for instance, can quickly turn into a meaningful budget line item (and add a ton of complexity) if your company grows to hundreds or thousands of employees. Likewise, the "soft costs" of programs are especially deceptive and easy to underestimate. Beyond just employee attention and administrative complexity, remember that every new program leaves your frontline managers in a potentially tough spot in determining how to implement and enforce added rules.[14]

Finally, correcting course on an already implemented program is difficult and can cause altogether new problems. Research suggests that the negative effects experienced when something is lost can be significantly stronger than the positive effects of receiving something of similar value.[15] In other words, canceling or reducing a popular program can have larger and longer-lasting negative impacts on morale than the originally intended benefits.[16] So, if you're thinking about offering free lunch every day when your company has fifty employees, you also need to be thinking about the fallout when you need to remove that benefit when your company has five hundred employees.

In summary, offering an excessively wide variety of supplementary programs is an all too common trap for high-growth organizations. Focus on the most fundamental benefits (i.e., health insurance), and hold off on others such as a 401(k), bonus plans, tuition reimbursement, or free lunch that do not meaningfully enhance your EVP. In the same spirit, actively work to avoid underestimating the snowball of costs (money, worker attention, administrative overhead, etc.) associated with new programs. If everything is in equal standing, opt for the simplest option. With these trade-offs in mind, several popular startup offerings may warrant critical evaluation and some skepticism (see table 4.1) as you think about ways to leverage your EVP.[17]

Table 4.1
Popular offerings that may not work for your startup

Offering	Your Employees Will Love It Because . . .	It Might Not Be Right for You Because . . .
Free lunches	People stay in the office over lunch, communicate with one another, and appreciate the free lunch.	There is really no such thing as a free lunch. The cost adds up quickly for employers (often $20/person/meal). Free lunches are shown not to drive employee satisfaction as much as traditional benefits such as health care, 401(k), or basic paid time off (PTO), so consider investing elsewhere first. If you decide free food is a must-have, we encourage clear guidelines and caution against daily offerings.
Happy hours	Free booze and fun, social atmosphere.	In this case, it is not about the cost as much as it is about the behavior being encouraged. Company sponsored happy hours have limited upside and tremendous downside (inappropriate behavior, drunk driving, exclusion of workers with limited scheduling flexibility, etc.). If you are determined to conduct after-hours social events, consider events that do not include alcohol (such as learning activities, trivia, or board games).

Executive coaches	Coaching shows a major investment in growth and development of participants.	At \$25,000 to \$100,000 per coaching participant per year, coaching is cost-prohibitive. That said, online coaching platforms such as Bravely, Betterup, and Sayge are beginning to gain traction. Compared to traditional coaching, their pricing is more accessible (\$3,000 to \$10,000 per year), and it may be possible to extend coaching beyond the executive team.
General leave programs	The number one motivator for some workers is time off.	These programs usually apply to less than 5 percent of employees at any given time. They can be especially costly for startups with short-tenured employees and high industry turnover rates. Unless there is a close connection to an organization's product or cultural identify, substitute a caregiver program such as Cleo or Care.com instead of offering additional paid leave.
Work from anywhere policies	Enhanced flexibility and some workers are more productive and satisfied.	Performance benefits are generally small. Perhaps more problematic, working relationships can suffer as a result of intense virtual work usage. In high-growth environments that demand adaptability and communication, having key members primarily working remotely can be detrimental to productivity. However, when considering access to a broader and potentially lower-cost labor pool, combined with lower facilities expenses, the trade-off may be worth considering. Public health issues represent obvious and important caveats to consider.
Unlimited paid time off (PTO)	Who wouldn't want unlimited paid vacation time?!	Make no mistake about it, unlimited PTO is not really intended to be unlimited. Rather, it was derived out of accounting rules that require any earned and accrued time that must be paid out at termination to be held as a financial liability on the books. Conversely, nonaccrued time that does not get paid out at employment termination is not considered an accounting liability. Loose (or no) guidelines regarding time off policies are an operational nightmare for managers to administer at growing companies. A more recently adopted term is "flexible time off," which is more accurate relative to the intent but has many of the same challenges. Both employees and managers generally prefer to know what the boundaries are, and there can be major legal and compliance risks related to managing any program without clear administrative rules. We typically suggest a simple PTO program offering federal holidays, several flexible personal days, sick time in accordance with the highest legal standard nationally, and vacation time of fifteen to twenty days for all workers.

Basic 4: Create an equity plan

An equity plan is an essential part of your minimum viable total rewards package from day one. In the early years of a startup, founders typically receive a negligible or nonexistent salary but take on meaningful ownership of the organization in return. In these scenarios, early equity agreements often emerge via handshake deals (e.g., "We're 50/50!"). Once the organization moves past the initial group of cofounders and starts hiring employees, the equity plan needs to be more formal than a handshake deal.

Strive to keep it simple—formal does not necessarily equal complicated! To help in this process, find a corporate attorney who specializes in startups. If they do not use a standard template, *find another lawyer*. Your equity plan should be clearly documented and relatively straightforward in the earliest days of your company's life cycle.

Most startup leaders are tempted to create an overly complex capitalization table with different terms and conditions for everyone. No matter what problems the bespoke approach solves in the short run, simplicity will save you headaches and money over time. For instance, capital partners typically expect a relatively "clean" capitalization table as a condition of investment, and they will consider the cost and effort required to buy out or normalize the equity terms of early shareholders in any investment offer. Furthermore, you should expect your early equity plan to last many years. Although you may periodically issue new shares, refresh the pool available for employee grants, or come up with an exceptional situation once every blue moon, those occasions will be rare (annually at most). Thus simplicity is a virtue.

Developing a reasonable equity plan requires a basic understanding of vehicle, vesting, and value. Most startups offer stock options that have a four-year vest period and a one-year cliff. This means that an employee earns the right to exercise 1/4 of the equity after one year and 1/48 of the total grant every month thereafter. Most organizations also offer "refresh grants" (postfunding) to employees who have been employed for a minimum of one to two years. These refresh grants are typically determined as a percentage of the new hire grant for an equivalent position and can be granted based solely on tenure or on outstanding performance or a recent promotion. In our experience, the vast majority of private venture-backed technology company startups use stock options as their only vehicle for employee equity grants and offer equity grants to all employees upon hire, regardless of title or level.

An obvious question is how much equity is the "right" amount? That answer will depend on the relative importance of the position as well as on the overall competitiveness you face for good candidates. If you cannot compete on cash compensation for a critical executive role or if the best talent is in short supply, you will need a lucrative equity plan. As your cash compensation approaches market pay, you can offer a more modest equity plan and lean more heavily on opportunities for growth and other elements of your EVP to lure good hires. Thankfully, there are several free benchmarking resources you can use to calibrate your offering. For example, both AngelList[18] and Wealthfront[19] offer interactive tools that allow you to compare compensation mixes across numerous filters (e.g., position level, geographic location). With new hire grant ranges typically adjusted after each capital raise, you should anticipate adjusting your benchmarks as you grow. We recommend Option Impact from Advanced HR[20] (free) for seed through Series B venture-backed companies and Radford's Private Company Survey[21] (which costs several thousand dollars) for companies that are at Series B or beyond.

Basic 5: Help your workers understand what's in it for them

So far, we have explained specific aspects of your company's minimum total viable rewards offering (equity, compensation, and other perks), which are the prerequisites of a strong EVP for most startups. Yet you must still refine and articulate that EVP by answering the "what's in it for me?" (WIIFM) question for current and prospective employees.

Workers intuitively evaluate whether they want to work for your company based on a long and complex set of subjective criteria, including (but not limited to) employer reputation, product branding, mission, geographic location, financial compensation, organizational stability, core benefits, career growth opportunities, performance expectations, values, and relationships with peers and management. Pay, equity plans, benefits, employee programs, and perks all play a significant role in that equation, but if your company cannot effectively communicate its broader EVP, their value is deeply discounted. Very much in the same way you need to make a compelling case to investors to raise growth capital, you also need to make a compelling case to attract and retain employees.

Understanding how all of these elements come together at your organization will help you more effectively attract and retain your targeted worker

Table 4.2
Programs and benefit distinctions

Startup	Mature Company
• Long work hours expected in a rapidly changing and highly innovative environment. • Prior industry experience is less relevant/valuable due to the disruptive nature of the product. • Career growth and personal development can be more rapid, although the organization is less stable. • Earlier career workers are more likely to perceive this environment as attractive.	• Complex but stable organization with highly sophisticated internal processes. • Consistent execution and learned skills are particularly critical, and retention of a stable, reliable workforce is prioritized over innovation. • Fewer new roles are being created than at a growth company, but personal and career development can be enhanced through structured training and rotational programs. • Later career workers are more likely to perceive this environment as attractive.

Generally Preferred Programs and Benefits	
Employee social events, career ladders with many rungs, and lifestyle programs/benefits will have great appeal. Medical insurance and retirement savings plans tend to be less valued by workers versus their relative administrative and financial costs.	Family leave programs, high quality and low employee contribution medical insurance, and retirement savings plans are likely to have great appeal. Programs such as social events may be perceived as less valuable to employees relative to alternatives.

population. Optimizing your time, effort, and resources requires ruthless prioritization of these programs. Start with a strong core package, then tailor your offerings to attract and retain the types of workers your organization most needs to succeed. Do not fool yourself into thinking that you can appeal to all audiences. The EVP at a small and growing organization is almost certainly quite different from the appeal of a larger, established company. Table 4.2 lists basic EVP distinctions between a startup and a mature company.

To effectively communicate an EVP, the "sell story" should be coordinated across the leadership team, hiring managers, and recruiters. This sell story should powerfully and accurately communicate the unique benefits and drawbacks of working for your organization. Without discriminating against any protected groups, you should set clear expectations about your organization and clearly explain the WIIFM. This allows candidates to self-select and commit strongly to the reality of your company if they choose to join. To avoid inadvertent unethical and unlawful discrimination, we encourage you to use broad underlying values that cut across different groups in your sell story (without intentionality, "fit" can be quickly bastardized).[22]

For example, describing an environment that is exciting (fast-paced, highly adaptive) and demanding (long hours) is accurate and could appeal to anyone. In contrast, saying we want employees with youthful energy and relatively few outside commitments says something altogether different and is not appropriate (i.e., we don't want "old" people with families). Table 4.3 provides two examples of how an EVP sell story can be tailored to specific company attributes. Resources ranging from pricey HR consulting services to free web-based templates[23] can help you distill your company's EVP.

Table 4.3
Sample EVP "sell stories"

Biotech Company	Business-to-Consumer Tech Company
• Employs a large contingent of specialized PhDs. Their schooling has typically been fully funded, so no need to offer student loan forgiveness. • A high percentage of PhDs in this field are conferred in schools outside the United States, therefore immigration support is essential. • Due to the length of school required, almost all qualified candidates will be thirty years of age or older. Given this demographic, health insurance and family-friendly programs (e.g., strong medical insurance for dependents, LTD/STD, and long-term care) will be more important compared to job listings that can be filled by a wider variety of employees, including candidates with less formal education (e.g., associate's or bachelor's degree holders). • The primary competition for these workers is academia, which offers highly stable but lower paying employment with the promise of tenure and a future pension. This company can either try to mirror that environment (which it could not effectively do at this stage of its life cycle) or directly oppose it with higher salaries and the upside of equity in trade for the lack of certainty in future employment.	• Employs many software engineers currently in high demand. Many of these workers have large student loans, so a loan forgiveness program is a tremendously attractive benefit. • The local market for software engineers is extremely competitive, but less so elsewhere. Therefore, the company may benefit from establishing an engineering office in another market (e.g., LATAM, Canada, university town in Midwest). • Most of the individuals with skills in the programming language this organization uses are recent college graduates. They primarily desire upward mobility, exposure to the latest technologies, and social engagement with their peers.

(continued)

Table 4.3   *(continued)*

Sample Sell Stories

"We are the opposite of university employment. We move fast, we innovate rapidly, and we're truly building something together. You will put in more hours than at a university, but you are paid handsomely for that time, and you participate in the potential upside of our business with an equity stake. We have very strong family-friendly benefits, including a full complement of insurance and savings programs, and you'll never have to write another grant request!"	"We offer the ideal environment for software engineers who want to grow their careers. We use the latest software languages, have social events every week, and more than half of our entry-level engineers are promoted within twelve months. Things move fast here, and you can anticipate long hours and changing priorities, but we set ourselves apart by paying off up to $10,000 of your student loans every year you are a part of our team."

One of the main reasons employees join (and stay at) any organization today is the opportunity for growth and development.[24] Particularly for startups, workers are so strongly motivated by the prospect of rapid advancement that they are willing to trade stability and security for the potential of accelerated career growth. As a result, many startups feel intense pressure from their employees to articulate "career ladders," providing as much detail as possible regarding the requirements to reach the next level of advancement. Although we discourage startups from spending time creating materials that are sure to be outdated before they are even printed, we recognize the strong desire from the workforce and the need to respond to those demands.

A preliminary step toward meeting this demand involves encouraging your managers to have meaningful, individualized conversations with their direct reports about employee opportunities for growth.[25] Beyond conversations, you can leverage existing generalized (cross-functional) frameworks for growth trajectories rather than creating your own specialized materials for each group within your company. Radford/Aon has developed the de facto standard for this space, with proprietary job leveling guides that are applicable across functions, job types, and career levels. You can gain access to their data and frameworks by participating in their surveys or engaging with their consulting team. Table 4.4 is a sample template that ties job levels to a compensation framework. Please note, base pay, bonus target, and new hire equity figures in the template are not intended to be recommendations—they are inserted only for illustrative purposes. Use figures based on appropriate benchmarks, and be aware that pay bands often overlap and that some individual contributor roles can be more highly compensated than managerial roles.

Table 4.4
Job levels connected to compensation ranges

[Department] Job Levels	Base Pay Range $	Bonus Target %	New Hire Equity (bps)	Typical Experience (years)	Management Responsibilities
Individual Contributor Level 1	70–85K	0	1	<2	No
Individual Contributor Level 2	75–90K	0	2	>1	No
Individual Contributor Level 3	80–110K	5	5	>2	No
Individual Contributor Level 4	100–130K	10	10	>4	Mentor
Individual Contributor Level 5	120–150K	15	20	>7	Mentor/Teach
Individual Contributor Level 6	150K+	20	30	>10	Mentor/Teach
Team Leader	90–125K	10	10	>5	Yes, IC Level 1–3
Manager	100–140K	15	15	>7	Yes, IC Level 1–4
Senior Manager	125–160K	20	20	>10	Yes, any above
Director	140–180K	25	25	>15	Yes, any above
Senior Director	165K–225K	30	40	>15	Yes, any above
Vice President	200K–275K	50	50	15+	Yes, any above

Conclusion

In the war for talent, many companies pull out all the stops to compete. This is a risky, often outright irresponsible game to play in the early stages of growth. Most startups do not have the resources to replicate the programs and perks of a Fortune 100 organization. Even if your organization does, offering a laundry list of programs will only dilute the EVP, resulting in inevitable administrative errors that hurt worker perceptions. Instead, value quality over quantity, and relentlessly communicate and reinforce your EVP. Focus first on the "table stakes" you need to stay in the conversation (your minimum viable total rewards policy), with particular emphasis on the areas where you can compete with (and even win against) your competitors (e.g., equity, growth environment, brand excitement). From there, leverage an expert to help you design, implement, and communicate a highly selective set of supplemental programs that appeal to your target employees. Be ruthless in your prioritization, avoid resource-draining programs with questionable returns, and stay clear of programs that cannot be reasonably scaled. An EVP is only valuable to the extent that it works for employees and your organization.

5

Learning and Development

Core and Strategic Investments

The first people/HR hire that we made at Pinterest—one of the highest growth companies of its time—was a learning and development leader. We were under one hundred employees, but we knew we had a strong trajectory going forward. The reason we did that is because we had assessed the talent base that we wanted to recruit and wanted to create a strong value proposition for those people. Value proposition is so, so important to attract and retain talent in a competitive labor market.

In terms of competition, we were recruiting most of our people from Facebook and Google. At the time, Google still offered "20 percent time," and much of it was being utilized for learning and development. Those companies also had massive learning and development infrastructure and real sophistication around their offerings, particularly for software engineers. And their talent brands were robust and compelling. To attract the talent we wanted, we needed to provide a competitive learning and development offering.

The employment social contract has evolved over time, particularly for knowledge workers. No longer is it compelling to simply accept steady wages in exchange for work. True job security is a thing of the past, so the workers are demanding more. We're now in a free agency environment, in which most people will spend only a few years with a given employer, particularly in the

fast-changing reality of high-growth technology companies. Knowledge is the currency of these workers' future
and their security going forward, so offering opportunities for real, valuable learning and development is critical
to the employment value proposition.

—CARA ALLAMANO, SVP OF PEOPLE, PLACES, AND
LEARNING AT UDEMY; FORMER SVP OF PEOPLE
AT PLANET; AND HEAD OF HUMAN RESOURCES
AT PINTEREST

The trigger for learning and development initiatives tends
to be when a company gets funding and opens a lot of
new jobs. The first thing those companies need to think
about is their new hire onboarding program. Often they
have existed for three or more years, they currently have
about fifty employees, and they hope to add another fifty
people in the next year. Growth at that pace is a great
opportunity, but it can be very dangerous and scary.
Founders can lose what they have built if they don't put
some structure around that growth and connecting their
new employees to the desired culture. It's a highly competitive job market. Candidates have a lot of choices, and
employer reputations are on the line with every new hire
experience. New hire onboarding needs to effectively
ramp up new employees, helping them find their footing at the organization and reach productivity. Usually, it
makes sense to start with a general new hire onboarding,
then tailor for major departments.

Sales training is usually another early focus. Building out
the sales team is typically where much of that new funding
is going, and it's easy to measure the return on that investment. Most sales teams would benefit more from support
than from how to prospect and how to handle objections.
The third priority tends to be management training, usually whenever a company is large enough to have a management layer. It's a major shift moving from buddy to
boss at a startup. There is also a lot of compliance training,
with requirements intensifying at fifty employees.

What should be on the short list, but often is not, is education about diversity, inclusion, and belonging in relation to the company culture. Verna Myers, VP of inclusion strategy at Netflix, positions this beautifully when she writes, "Diversity is being asked to the party. Inclusion is being asked to dance." And I have heard added, "Belonging is having your song played." In a tight labor market with a diverse millennial population, employers must pay attention to these issues, intentionally building diversity, inclusion, and belonging practices into their overall culture through learning and other initiatives in the business.

It's also critical to sponsor broader learning and development opportunities throughout the organization. The number one reason people choose to join companies now is their perception of professional growth opportunities there. It's not just money. It's not ping-pong. It's because they think they can grow through the experience at that company.

—KATI RYAN, FOUNDER OF A POSITIVE ADVENTURE

CHAPTER 5 RUNDOWN

The Problem
Many workers expect rapid skill and career growth, which can seem misaligned with your current needs and resources.

The Plan
Determine the most critical needs, and focus relentlessly on execution.

The Basics
1. Invest in the common core offerings.
2. Layer in only a few high-impact programs and squash the rest.
3. Say "no" or "not yet" to everything else.
4. Determine execution strategy.

The Problem

You have been fortunate enough to recruit some talented employees, and their pay and benefits requirements have been effectively addressed.

However, in part due to the competitive nature of your local market for talent, not all of these employees are experienced in their craft. Many people are in more complex roles than they have held in the past, and you are particularly worried about the many first-time people managers. You recognize that you have critical product, engineering, and marketing activities owned by people who are undeniably bright and motivated but not necessarily hitting the ground running. They are not always working on the things you think are most important, and they seem to demand a new social, cultural, or developmental program every day.

Learning and development programs are not just a "nice to have" but are a "must have" in today's hypercompetitive talent environment. Speaking to this point, renowned HR expert Josh Bersin writes, "Companies that can rapidly develop new skills internally will far outperform their peers. It's no longer possible to 'hire' your way to success: your most powerful strategy for business growth is to build skills from within."[1] But how do you know which learning initiatives you should provide? How will you deliver them? And how will you know if they are working?

The Plan

When thinking about learning and development programs, be mindful of the possibility of getting lost by pursuing too many overlapping initiatives. Even if well intentioned, doing so is problematic because it confuses employees and obfuscates measures of impact, which may explain why data collected by McKinsey indicated that a majority of employees see training programs as misaligned with business priorities and failing to add substantive value.[2] Steve Glaveski, CEO of Collective Campus, recently lamented that employees often learn the wrong things at the wrong times and end up forgetting any potentially useful information as a result.[3] In the same vein, Laszlo Bock, founder of Humu and former Google executive, argues that "you learn best when you learn less."[4]

Mountains of programs are available, but only a few "common core" learning and development programs are critical for most startups. To get the most impact for your dollar, concentrate the bulk of your time and resources on the essential programs and selectively invest in just a few additional offerings that supplement your company's EVP and workforce planning goals. To guide your investment decisions, first identify the broad problems or areas of opportunity (e.g., revenue, delivery times, customer satisfaction, employee turnover) that, if addressed, will push you toward a more competitive positioning.[5] Once you have determined the highest leverage areas, capture the current performance baseline, look for commonsense interventions you can reasonably apply, and measure changes in behaviors and actual business outcomes. Participation rates and satisfaction scores are rarely adequate measures of a program's performance.[6]

After selecting a short list of areas to address and deciding how to measure the impact of your efforts, the next challenge is figuring out how to best deliver on those needs. Your company can choose to build, rent, or buy training content and employee development *frameworks*; and you can build, rent, or buy the *capability* to deliver that *content* (e.g., stand-up trainers, online classes, quick reference guides). Founders tend to have a natural inclination to build content unique to their company or thoughtlessly replicate another organization's program, but this is rarely the optimal choice. In the overwhelming majority of cases, your company's learning needs are not unique, and there are preexisting methods for accomplishing them. Early on, your default position as a small to midsized business should be to buy or rent the majority of training content and delivery infrastructure, with only a few exceptions. You will still need to be wary of internal empire builders and hungry external vendors when choosing your delivery methods, of course, but staying away from the "build" option in most cases will save tremendous time, headaches, and eventually money. Remember, walking through a slide deck in a conference room is not training, it is just a presentation. True learning and development programs are designed for how people learn and retain information. Kati Ryan, founder of A Positive Adventure, tells us, "If developing thorough training was easy, you are probably doing it wrong." Working with real professionals to design the content and think through the delivery can improve the likelihood that your training programs accomplish what is intended rather than wasting time and money.

The Basics

Basic 1: Invest in the common core offerings

Across business models, geographies, and maturity stages, high-growth startups have at least one key thing in common: rapid headcount expansion. Consequently, the most pressing common core learning and development programs usually spring naturally from the following needs:

(1) select/assess job candidates, (2) onboard and orient new hires, and (3) establish and communicate expectations for new managers.

Many of the learning needs associated with selection are implied in chapter 3. Generally, the training involved in selection skills can be condensed into an overview of the selection/assessment process and a walk-through of existing structured interview guides for those who will participate as hiring managers or members of an interview panel. This training can be somewhat informal if the selection process is reasonably well-defined and interview guides exist for most roles. Common topics include basic but nevertheless critical issues such as how to open an interview (research suggests that pre-interview chit chat can bias interview outcomes),[7] sticking to the script when asking questions, active listening and note-taking techniques, limiting probing questions (and avoiding leading questions), and scoring each response timely and appropriately rather than scoring all responses at the end of the interview.[8] As you discuss topics with hiring managers, be aware that some may dismiss the information as HR mumbo-jumbo. For those people, it may help to emphasize that research clearly suggests the superiority of structured interview techniques over less formal methods and, equally important, that experienced hiring managers (even those calling themselves "experts") are notoriously poor at making the "right" choices based on their intuition and gut.[9] If structured interview guides do not yet exist for the roles you are trying to fill, this gap should be closed in partnership between the talent acquisition team and the department head before pursuing broader-based interview training.

New employees are almost constantly entering growth-oriented startups and will lean heavily on your existing employees, especially managers, as they make their transition from organizational outsiders to insiders.[10] In general, newcomers are disproportionately likely to leave an organization within their first few months, and if they stay, it can take upward of a year to fully ramp up in a new role.[11] Some practitioners estimate that the cost of replacing newcomers (e.g., recruiting and training a replacement, resetting the ramp-up clock) is about two times the role's initial salary.[12] Given the constrained resources and breakneck speed of a growing startup, this is simply not tenable.

On the upside, a vast amount of research clearly suggests that organizations that mindfully and intentionally onboard newcomers through the socialization process can dramatically improve newcomer adjustment and success rates.[13] Alas, new managers charged with onboarding new employees often grossly underestimate the amount of time and effort required to effectively onboard newcomers. One helpful framework for thinking about successful onboarding is the "4 C's:" compliance, clarification, culture, and connection.[14] The more you can build up a newcomer's understanding and fit with each of the C's, the better. In other words, signing all the legal paperwork on Day 1 is a requisite but not sufficient criteria. For startups that cannot afford lengthy and formalized onboarding programs, we recommend first implementing a relatively brief program to take care of the main compliance issues and to provide newcomers with other information regarding company- and department-specific indoctrinations (some of this should have been shared during the recruitment and selection process). At a minimum, the company-wide component should include:

- Organizational overview (leadership team; high-level organizational chart; company history; mission, vision, and values; company goals, explanation of the company's products and services, etc.)
- Instructions on accessing company services (technology, facilities, HR, accounting, directory, Slack, intranet, help desk, etc.)
- Information about cross-company tools and processes (performance reviews, employee surveys, training and development programs, meeting and communication venues, employee policies such as travel and expenses, and time and attendance, etc.)

The department or team-level version of onboarding should include:

- Department/team overview (roles and responsibilities of subteams, possibly a RACI chart, organization chart, goals and major initiatives, etc.)
- Information about department/team tools and processes (walk-through of project management and collaboration tools, meeting cadence, etc.)
- Information about role expectations for the newcomer
- Introduction to key stakeholders

As you might expect, newcomers will be overwhelmed in their first few days on the job, so managers need to check in regularly and continue to be active in guiding the newcomer's socialization into the company. For example, managers should schedule one-on-ones with people with whom the new hire most closely works, identify possible mentorship partners, and arrange periodic skip-level meetings with next-level managers to give the newcomer more perspective on the culture and to build meaningful connections in the organization. Relatively inexperienced managers may feel pressure to treat newcomer onboarding as a two- or three-day event that everyone must endure before returning to their "normal" jobs. This is a shortsighted view that will ultimately cost the organization time and money down the road. Stress the importance of effective onboarding and the value of managers' continued involvement with newcomers, and work to build in managerial bandwidth for these activities.[15]

Finally, periodic manager training is necessary to support newly promoted or hired managers as well as to reinforce expectations for existing managers. This manager training should dive deeper into the mission, vision, values, and goals of the organization than broad-based communications to an all-employee audience allows, providing richer context on performance management, feedback, and goal-setting processes that exist at the organization. In some instances, providing more information about business planning and budgeting, recruitment and selection, and related topics may add value. In short, your goal is to help your managers serve as the primary spokespeople to their teams for the organization's foundational systems and, where needed, to act autonomously in ways that support the organization's mission. To build an empowered team of managers, you must share enough strategic information so managers can understand why certain programs exist and provide a psychologically safe context in which managers can ask pointed questions.[16]

Basic 2: Layer in a few high-impact offerings and squash the rest

Pay, benefits, and perks are only part of the equation for attracting and retaining skilled workers in the war for talent. Workers also see significant value in learning and development programs that prepare them for advancement and future opportunities. To avoid program bloat (and all of the administrative costs and confusion that come with it), startups must be highly selective in using their limited resources to invest in *only a few* programs that will truly move the needle for their employees and their company. Table 5.1 outlines some common training and development programs that are typically good investments for startups, and others that can usually wait.

In a classic high-growth startup environment, a company is based in a high-cost urban center and employs mostly early-career skilled workers in a competitive labor market. This environment demands outsized investments in frontline manager training, career development, and

Table 5.1
Good and poor training investments for high-growth startups

Good Investment	Poor Investment
New employee orientation	Team building
Frontline manager skills training	Internship and rotational programs
Executive coaching (on a limited basis)	Technical job skill training
Goal clarification and communication	Internally created soft skills training content
Basic process checklists and process maps	Highly detailed job descriptions
Self-service employee resource guides (e.g., wiki)	Company-specific career ladders

personal development. However, the training needs change in environments in which the talent market may be less competitive or less skilled (focus shifts to formal training). Thus the geographic footprint (among other factors) of a startup determines the nature of the "training tax" incurred to deliver maximum value. Keeping the broader talent context in mind is crucial for identifying the highest leveraged learning and development opportunities for your organization.

Progressive and innovative programs are best saved for well-established organizations that are now trying to differentiate themselves from other mature entities. A startup organization is already differentiated by being high growth and in a state of rapid change. Do not waste limited attention and resources on nonessential programs or in time-consuming areas that are very likely to change substantially in the near future.

Even when a leader is aware of current priorities, it can be tremendously challenging to tactfully deny suggestions or requests from passionate team members. Will they become disgruntled and leave if you do not pursue their request? Do you truly support their idea and think it would be a fun thing to try? Whatever the hesitation, you must actively avoid the pitfall of passively deflecting these requests with statements such as "go ahead and run with that." Sure, you may get lucky; the employee may lack the energy to pursue the idea further, but in many cases they will not. After only a few undisciplined responses, you and your organization will be juggling a multitude of half-baked and disconnected programs that quickly absorb an untold amount of time from some of your most valuable and motivated people.

Team members may be enthusiastic about a passion project today, but that does not mean it is a good use of their time and attention.

As a high-profile example, Google's famous "20 percent time" policy sounded like a great idea to drive creativity, and many employees loved it. But, by and large, it did not work and was ultimately abandoned.[17] Every time you get a request, ask yourself if the initiative will add real value beyond change. If the answer is "no"—and it most often is given your organization's positioning—do not agree to one-off personal requests. You probably do not have the resources of Google or Facebook and, consequently, cannot support the same range of programs they offer or afford to absorb a failed experiment. Therefore, you must kindly (but clearly) kill most well-intentioned program requests through direct discussions. The following list provides some sample discussions you can use to guide your approach in these tough but deceptively crucial conversations.

SAMPLE TRAINING REQUEST DIALOGUES

EXAMPLE 1

Top Engineer: I think we should start a mentoring program to help new hires get up to speed faster.

You: Wow, I really appreciate the idea! Our primary focus right now is accelerating our progress against the product road map. I can see how getting new hires up to speed better and faster could potentially do that. However, we already have a robust orientation program, and each hiring manager is expected to complete a ninety-day plan for their new hires. What gap in our existing programs would this idea address?

Top Engineer: Well, I'm not really sure. I just know that the new engineer on XYZ's team is struggling, and I think that we need to help him.

You: It sounds like the best solution here might be for XYZ to really dig in to help her new hire. Have you spoken with her yet?

Top Engineer: No, I didn't want to embarrass her, and she is so overwhelmed that I think XYZ just doesn't have time to help her new hire enough.

You: I really appreciate you bringing this up. I'd like you to chat with XYZ directly about this, and maybe you can help somehow. It sounds like we don't necessarily need a company-wide mentoring program—we just need to make sure that our hiring managers prioritize new employee onboarding.

EXAMPLE 2

New Director of Marketing: I think we should start a lunch and learn program here. Each department can talk about what they're working on, teams will get to know each other better, and we can highlight wins across the company. We did it at my last company, and people really enjoyed it.

You: Thanks for the suggestion! Our primary focus right now is [unrelated to this idea], but we're always trying to make this a great place to work and to encourage cross-team collaboration. I could see this being fun and interesting, but I also don't want to create more program management work for team members that isn't directly related to our primary focus. Let's hold off on any new programs until things stabilize (next round of funding, major goal reached, etc.), but as a new hire it could be great for you to get to know some of the key people around here and what they do. Tell you what, your next business lunch will be on me. Go ahead and invite a few people you don't know and try to come away with a better understanding of who does what.

EXAMPLE 3

Associate Product Manager: I think we should have more detailed job descriptions and career ladders here to know what our responsibilities are and exactly what it takes to get promoted.

You: Thanks a lot for the suggestion! Our primary focus right now is [unrelated to this idea], but we're always trying to make this a great place to work and to encourage development. I could see how a lot of people would value clarity about job responsibilities and career progression. Have you talked about this with your manager or department head?

Associate Product Manager: Yes, during my last performance review. I didn't get promoted, but I thought that I should have. I've already been here thirteen months! My manager told me that HR controls the job descriptions, and we don't have a career ladder. She told me that I should talk to HR or to you to figure out what it takes to be promoted.

You: Wow, it sounds like your manager could have owned this topic better. We have some good basic job descriptions, but you know that they will never be able to capture every detail of everything that people are responsible for in the moment. That's true even at very large and stable companies. It's important that managers are in constant communication with their team members to ensure that responsibilities and expectations are clear. I expect you and your manager to be having one-on-ones at least weekly, despite your job description not being updated each time.

Your manager is also right that we don't have a formal or detailed career ladder yet. It's still a judgment call by each manager when to propose that someone be promoted. That judgment call should be based on a combination of skills, experience, and sustained performance. Department heads review those recommendations, and both HR and I then look at anything that a department head supports. This comes back to you and your manager having good conversations about expectations. I know that your manager is [new/busy], but this is something that you can drive with her as well. I love that you're ambitious and looking to grow in your career, so go ahead and take the reins. Have a conversation with her about expectations, and write down a list of things you can do and demonstrate for her to feel comfortable recommending you for a promotion. Send me an email after you have that list—I'd love to see it!

Some common themes emerge in employees' learning and development requests. However, program requests are often related to individual situations and are better addressed through a candid discussion with a manager or a peer. Similarly, program requests may pop up due to a gap in execution or capability. Startup leaders must learn to directly address the communication, execution, and capability gaps without being ensnared by supporting ancillary programs that suck time and attention from the broader organization—training is not a panacea for fixing all issues.[18] We recommend using a "know, willing, able" framework[19] to diagnose whether a problem can be reasonably addressed by training (see table 5.2). If a problem

Table 5.2
Know, willing, able analysis

Know	Does the individual know what to do in the given situation? (skill, instructions)
Willing	Is the individual willing to do what is required?
Able	Are there any obstacles to the individual performing the desired behavior (equipment, competing priorities, conflicting metrics, approval process, etc.)?

can be traced to employees' knowledge or skills (i.e., "know"), then training may be a suitable approach. If not, the problem may be more closely related to employee motivation (i.e., willing) or underlying operational issues (i.e., "able") that will not be sufficiently addressed by a training program.

Basic 3: Measure the impact

Unfortunately, the most convenient indicators of program success, such as completion rates and participant satisfaction, are also the weakest.[20] If you are considering a major program, we suggest first identifying the business performance metric you hope to move (e.g., revenue per salesperson per quarter, tickets resolved per week per IT support administrator, customer satisfaction score, new hire turnover after ninety days, etc.). If you do not have a precise, value-adding metric available for pre- and posttraining comparisons, it will be nearly impossible to understand the return on investment or whether the training is accomplishing what was originally intended. In the same vein, overlapping training and development interventions also cloud your ability to understand what worked and what did not, thereby making future training investment decisions difficult.

A relatively simple way to avoid wasting employee time and company dollars is to run a basic control group exercise in which the learning/development intervention is applied to only a portion of the target population. This allows you to filter out the noise of ongoing changes at a rapidly evolving organization and make a clearer case for or against a program's impact. If the intervention is successful, you can easily roll out the program to others. If not, you can evaluate other options. Table 5.3 and figure 5.1 demonstrate such an impact analysis.

Table 5.3
Sample training program impact analysis (in percent)

	90-Day Retention	<1 Year Retention	Participant Survey	<1 Year Engagement
Four-month average prior to program	90	82	n/a	67
Q1 rolling twelve-month average	100	80	85	75
Q2 rolling twelve-month average	85	83	88	68
Q3 rolling twelve-month average	91	78	82	76
Q4 rolling twelve-month average	94	85	90	82

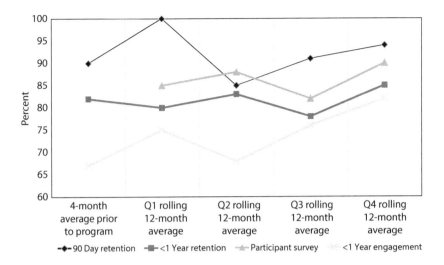

Figure 5.1
Sample training program impact analysis

Many startups take a shortcut, broadly executing programs that leaders intuitively and earnestly believe to be "the right thing to do," even though no clear business rationale has been identified. The value proposition of these programs is highly debatable, and they are frequently challenged when leadership turns over or when something new becomes the next "right thing." Until your organization has firmer footing as a business, we urge caution and restraint when evaluating programs that do not have a clear connection to business outcomes. Remember, your organization can build and value many virtues outside of formal training programs.

Basic 4: Determine execution strategy

Once you have selected the most impactful areas to address and determined the metrics you will use to assess impact, you need to figure out how to execute these new initiatives. Many founders have a bias toward believing that their organization is unique—completely different from all other organizations—and as a result, they encourage the creation of content and programs to suit their perceived unique needs. They also have a bias toward developing internal delivery capabilities, avoiding vendor fees, and trusting team members over "outsiders who don't know us."

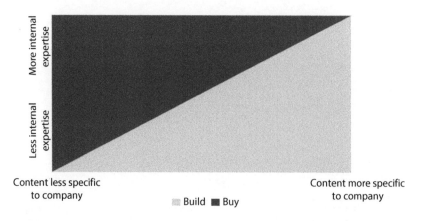

Figure 5.2
Build versus buy analysis

Table 5.4
Build versus buy decisions by program or tool

Program/Tool	Internal Expertise	Context Specific to Company	Build/Buy Decision
New employee orientation	High	High	Build
Frontline manager skills training	Low	Low	Buy/rent
Executive coaching	Low	Low	Buy/rent
Goal clarification and communication	High	High	Build
Basic process checklists and process maps	High	High	Build
Self-service employee resource guides (e.g., wiki)	High	High	Build
Team building	Low	Low	Buy/rent
Internship and rotational programs	Low	Depends	Depends
Lunch and learn	High	High	Build
Technical job skill training	Depends	Low	Buy/rent
Soft skills training (communications, feedback)	Low	Low	Buy/rent

It is true that each organization is different and special, but any given company is rarely *unique enough* to avoid outsourcing options (a rare exception is some portion of newcomer onboarding content).[21] Figure 5.2 diagrams the build versus buy paradigm, and table 5.4 outlines some common programs and the appropriate build versus buy decision for *most* resource-constrained startups.

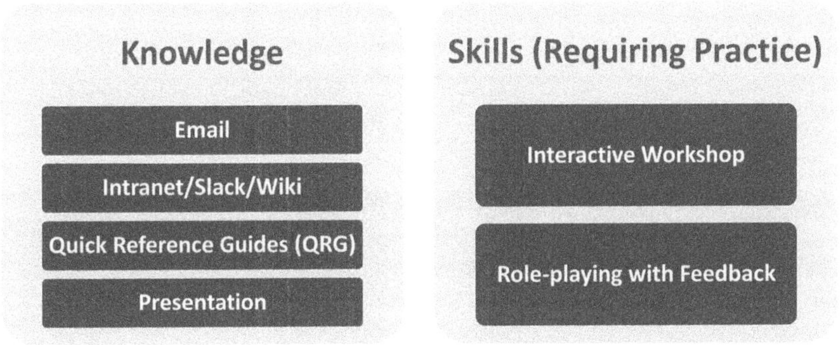

Figure 5.3
Preferred content delivery methods (one-way for knowledge; two-way for skills)

Table 5.5
Learning type by common program/tool

Program/Tool	Primary Learning Type
New employee orientation	Knowledge
Frontline manager skills training	Skills
Executive coaching	Skills
Goal clarification and communication	Knowledge
Basic process checklists and process maps	Knowledge
Self-service employee resource guides (e.g., wiki)	Knowledge
Team building	Skills
Internship and rotational programs	Skills
Lunch and learn	Knowledge
Technical job skill training	Knowledge
Soft skills training (communications, feedback)	Skills

It is not surprising that research supports the idea that the effectiveness of training delivery methods varies based on the type of knowledge or skill you are trying to build.[22] A general rule of thumb we follow is that self-study and one-way communication techniques are most appropriate when acquiring knowledge, and more interactive two-way communication techniques are best for building skills that require practice (see figure 5.3). Using this basic framework can save hours of unnecessary classroom training and enable your team to build the targeted skills more effectively. Table 5.5 provides some examples of how to apply this litmus test.

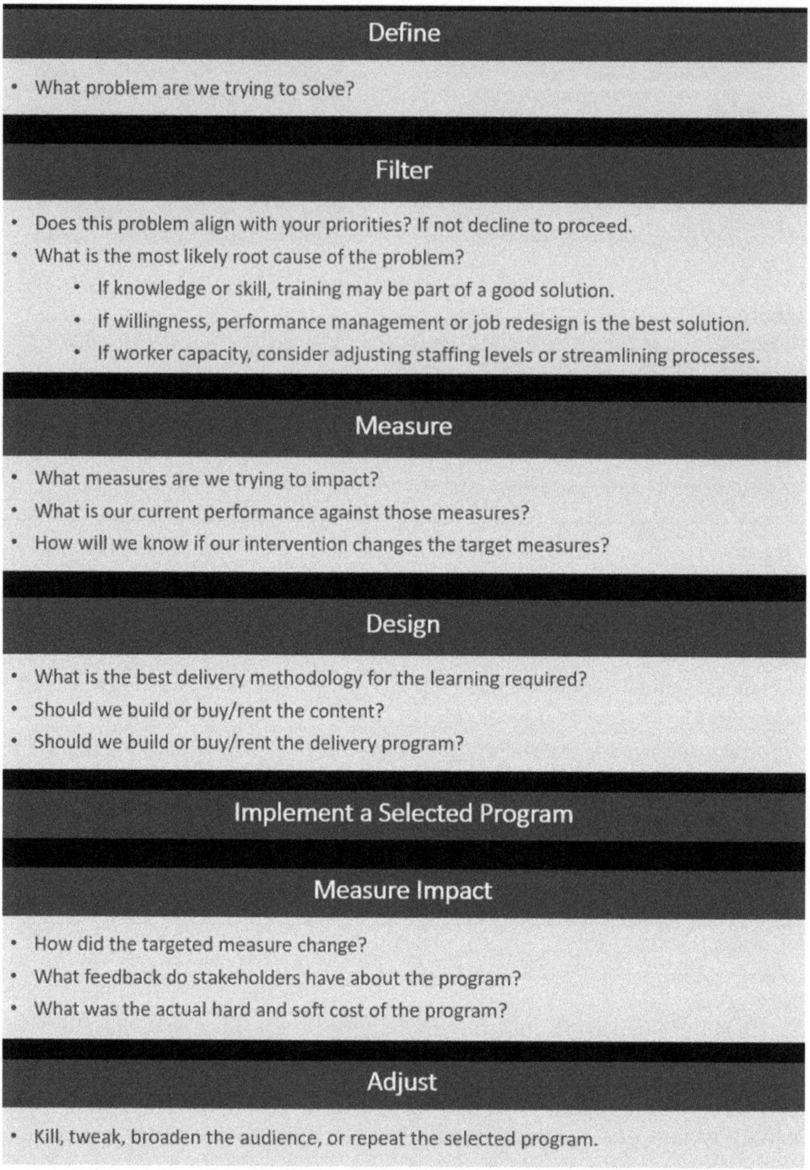

Define

- What problem are we trying to solve?

Filter

- Does this problem align with your priorities? If not decline to proceed.
- What is the most likely root cause of the problem?
    - If knowledge or skill, training may be part of a good solution.
    - If willingness, performance management or job redesign is the best solution.
    - If worker capacity, consider adjusting staffing levels or streamlining processes.

Measure

- What measures are we trying to impact?
- What is our current performance against those measures?
- How will we know if our intervention changes the target measures?

Design

- What is the best delivery methodology for the learning required?
- Should we build or buy/rent the content?
- Should we build or buy/rent the delivery program?

Implement a Selected Program

Measure Impact

- How did the targeted measure change?
- What feedback do stakeholders have about the program?
- What was the actual hard and soft cost of the program?

Adjust

- Kill, tweak, broaden the audience, or repeat the selected program.

Figure 5.4
Training program life-cycle flowchart

Conclusion

Learning and development can be vital to retaining talent and maximizing it, particularly for early-career individuals and those in first-time managerial roles. Startup leaders often are best served to focus on core programs plus a very select offering of other programs that appeal to employees and add business value. In the same spirit, leaders must be vigilant to avoid building too many custom programs and delivering too many of those programs inefficiently (typically overusing classroom training). Figure 5.4 provides a training life-cycle flowchart for navigating these decisions.

When a high-growth business tries to take on more than it can handle with scarce resources, it is flirting with outright disaster. Remember, not every issue can be solved with training. You must filter requests, forget keeping up with the Joneses, and invest where you get a positive return on investment (validated by calculating the return on investment and evaluating it against other opportunity costs). If you decide training is needed, but that need is not unique to your organization (as is frequently the case), relying on outside experts, frameworks, and materials can help you generate faster, cheaper, and better results. We particularly encourage early-stage startups to engage with vendors willing to work closely as a partner with them, delivering both expertise and high-quality content and tailoring that content to meet the specific needs of the business.

6

Culture, Engagement, and Communications

Creating the Environment for Success

In my twenty-plus years of consulting to founders, CEOs, and leaders, I've found that in the most vibrant and thriving organizations the "how" of their culture has a different level of urgency and importance than it does in less vibrant organizations. In thriving organizations, culture is not relied on to play defense but rather offense. It's not a passive force but an active discipline with a set of deliberate practices and mindsets. Their culture doesn't preserve the organization from the forces of change but makes it resilient, adaptable, and always moving forward. It is not taken for granted but is relied upon to develop people, overcome setbacks, beat competitors, execute strategy, and innovate.

Those organizations see "what" they do or make as an important tactical challenge, but they believe it's not enough to do "what" exceptionally well in order to succeed. Why not? Because "what" can change at the drop of a hat. Markets shift. Competition gets crowded. Technology alters the game that's being played. If "what" is all you know how to do, then you're likely to continue struggling to do that particular thing even when it no longer makes sense. In contrast, if "how" is the source of your resiliency and growth, then you are more likely to

know when change and innovation are needed and may
even have a good inkling of what needs to be done next.
—SARA ROBERTS, ENTREPRENEUR, EXECUTIVE
ADVISOR, AND AUTHOR OF *NIMBLE, FOCUSED, FEISTY:
ORGANIZATIONAL CULTURES THAT WIN IN THE NEW ERA
AND HOW TO CREATE THEM*

CHAPTER 6 RUNDOWN

The Problem
As you grow, the culture changes whether you like it or not.

The Plan
Determine the cultural attributes that matter most, then align your communications and ways of working with those attributes.

The Basics
1. Honor the best of the past while embracing the future.
2. Define a clear and differentiated culture.
3. Be yourself.
4. Align programs to support your desired culture.
5. Ensure good two-way communication.

The Problem

Your company has grown so much that employees now work from home
or across multiple office locations, sometimes even across time zones.
You have hired excellent department heads and managers, and your
product has real traction in the market. At the same time, you feel like
you are losing connection with the work and your growing team. You
used to see everyone most days, but now you are not even interviewing
every person that gets hired. Often you go long periods of time without
having a meaningful conversation with your employees. Your anxiety
ramps up as you are forced to trust people you barely know to make
good decisions while getting things done the way you would want them
to be done.

Beyond your personal struggles, you also realize that most of these people do not know *you* either. They certainly observe what you say and do (or
do not say and do) from afar, but most people do not get one-on-one time
with you. As a result, you start to see or hear about increased misunderstandings, more disgruntled employees, a more active rumor mill, and frequently
missed goals. This is not just an operational problem; this is a *culture* problem.

The Plan

Culture is an inherently messy concept that influences and is influenced
by myriad factors, which from an academic perspective has created long-
standing definitional challenges (e.g., everyone has their own definition).[1]
For our purposes, we use a description advanced by Harvard professor
Boris Groysberg and his coauthors: "Culture expresses goals through values and beliefs and guides activity through shared assumptions and group
norms."[2] Therefore, culture is less about what you say and more about what
you do. Despite how many companies treat building a culture, it is more
than just organizing happy hours, hanging posters, and providing progressive perks. Culture is rooted in how people are rewarded, recognized, promoted, and fired; it reflects the "correct way to perceive, think, and feel" in
a particular organization.[3]

A healthy culture pushes the organization to work on the right things,
get those things done, and repeat those activities with a sustainable level
of internal friction (e.g., constructive interactions). Many startups strive
to establish a culture that attracts risk-tolerant, skilled workers. To do this,
they often provide workers with the most flexibility and the most development and career-growth opportunities that they can possibly deliver.
Broadly speaking, this is a reasonably effective 80/20 approach for many
startups, particularly those centered in highly competitive labor markets
(e.g., San Francisco Bay area). Yet several pitfalls can cause well-intentioned
culture-building efforts to become happy hour memes that are remarkably
ineffective in attracting, retaining, and utilizing talent.

Building and reinforcing a healthy culture requires leaders to recon-
cile their organization's past with its future, with the goal of identifying any
unique cultural attributes worth preserving. Likewise, because organizational
growth comes with new employees, new structures, and new programs that
ultimately affect how employees experience their organizational lives, leaders
must work relentlessly to align their management decisions and practices with

the organization's desired culture. Related to this aim, establishing rich two-way communication channels is imperative for maintaining and improving company culture. We address each of these basics in the following section.

The Basics

Basic 1: Honor the best of the past while embracing the future

When a startup is created, its culture is largely based on the founder's (or founding team's) personality and working tendencies.[4] Initially, founders have direct, often intensely personal relationships with all employees, and the company's work processes are often direct reflections of a founder's preferences. Inevitably the context will change over time (often both externally and internally),[5] thereby making the culture less a direct result of the founder's personal influence as the number of employees expands. Research suggests that most individuals cannot maintain more than about 150 relationships ("Dunbar's Number").[6] In addition, the emotional depth of these relationships is, on average, lower as individuals approach the upper limits of that boundary.[7] Extrapolated to startups, leaders cannot rely solely on their personal reach to affect all employees because they (and their employees) simply do not have the bandwidth to deeply connect with everyone else. Thus leaders concerned about driving a healthy culture must be thoughtful about their *indirect* influences as much or more so than their direct influences.

The shifts from a founding team of two to five people, to a funded team of about twenty people, to a scaling team of one-hundred-plus people and beyond are intense for everyone, but especially for the founding team. Founders are often brilliant, driven, and successful in many ways, but they tend to be overly reliant on old practices that worked at an earlier stage of the company's life cycle that are no longer relevant for—and often detrimental to—future success.

For example, dominant CEOs/founders will often implement draconian measures to try to maintain absolute control of the many activities occurring throughout the growing business, thereby disempowering other leaders and discouraging workers from responding adaptively to the environment. A culture that was once efficient and execution-driven soon becomes stifling and unrewarding at scale. Conversely, more fluid, relationship-based (usually accountability averse) CEOs/founders will allow their organization to drift from one great speech to another without delivering meaningful clarity or reliable expectations. In this case, the culture inspired by leadership shifts from inspiring and purpose-driven to frustrating and cynical.

Founders and early employees may cling to suboptimal historical practices during growth for any number of reasons, including a natural tendency to revert to old behaviors under stress (i.e., threat rigidity)[8] or mistakenly attributing the causes of prior success. An essential ingredient for healthy growth is the willingness to change, and the best organizations navigate culture change by honoring the best of the past in ways that promote adaptability toward a better future. One way to walk this line is to take charge of and leverage storytelling as an agent of culture change.[9] Stories allow you to acknowledge what has happened previously and to decode those events in a way that highlights an underlying value rather than a particular practice that is no longer viable. To be sure, some stories will persist whether the organization's leadership wants them to or not (another reason to avoid excessive happy hours). However, leadership can selectively amplify stories that will resonate with employees and reinforce the desired culture. For example, if a founder started out having one-on-ones every week with each employee, an organization could continue to highlight that effort as folklore indicative of the overall organization's belief that communication with frontline employees is critical. New arrangements, including midlevel manager check-ins with employees or even once a month town halls with the CEO, are still compatible with early employees' visions of the company's origins.

Basic 2: Define a clear and differentiated culture

Very much related to the previous point, you need to clearly articulate your desired culture to existing team members and candidates before you can align programs and processes. Carmela Krantz, founder of Woven HR and multiple-time head of people, believes that "people want to work at a place where they understand their value and how their work is connected to the company's mission and vision. Great people practices support the company in every aspect of scaling."

Everyone wants to work somewhere with a "great culture," but that means different things to different people. Unfortunately, you cannot be everything to everyone, so high-growth leaders need to engage in a thoughtful and intentional decision about what cultural values they want to highlight without losing sight of their actual business. Despite the prevalence of "culture talk" in popular startup discourse, many startup leaders avoid intentional culture-refining activities entirely. We can only speculate on why this is so. One possibility is that startup leaders have seen other companies fall into time-sucking black holes working to generate ultimately bland mission, vision, and values statements. We get it—many mission statements miss the mark, and wasted time is debilitating for growth-oriented startups. Yet there are simpler, less time-consuming ways to determine the cultural values that make the most sense for you to reinforce.

Start by scrapping the typical mission, vision, and values statement generation process and focus on just two big questions: (1) Why does our organization exist (purpose)? and (2) What are our strongest *and most unique* behavioral characteristics (behaviors)? *Purpose* is akin to *mission*, but using a different term will help you ward off the temptation to borrow from a hodgepodge of other company statements. Similarly, *behaviors* are akin to *values*, but thinking in terms of behaviors will help your team avoid lofty platitudes and instead find actionable things that can be used to inform employee expectations.[10] Somewhat controversially, we suggest skipping *vision* entirely. A vision for a high-growth company is usually too future-oriented, ambiguous, and unpredictable to be useful.

As you begin discussing your purpose (mission) and behaviors (values), use the following guidelines to keep your team pulling in the same direction:

1. Answers should be candidate/employee-facing (rather than customer-facing).
2. Avoid jargon or acronyms and keep the output short and simple (shorter is better).
3. List no more than five behaviors/values that are truly special in your organization (anything more dilutes the message).
4. Purpose statements need to be unquestionably clear and straightforward. Attempts at mass appeal will likely have the least appeal, so seek out unique attributes.

The following list provides sample statements, and table 6.1 has an exercise to further uncover your company's purpose.

MISSION/PURPOSE STATEMENT EXAMPLES

1. We sell soda (Pepsi)
2. Celebrating animals, confronting cruelty (Humane Society)
3. Use our imaginations to bring happiness to millions (Disney)

Table 6.1

Uncovering your organizational purpose exercise

Question 1: Simply, what does our business do?	
Sample Answer (for real estate tech company): We buy, remodel, rent, and manage homes.	
2a: What's the benefit of that?	More professional management and maintenance
(repeat this question until you arrive at the simplest viable option)	Better rental property at a reasonable price
2b: What's the benefit of that?	No dependence on "mom and pop" part-time landlords
	Higher-quality rental experience
2c: What's the benefit of that?	Saves time, increase convenience
2d: What's the benefit of that?	Reduces stress
	More time to enjoy life and family
Sample Purpose Statements	We make renting easy.
	We make a house your home.

Note: This exercise is intended to elicit language that will elevate your organization's purpose to be both accurate and inspirational.

4. Nourishing families so they can flourish and thrive (Kellogg)
5. Improving the lives of the world's consumers, now and for generations to come (Procter & Gamble)
6. Creating insanely great products (Apple)
7. Embracing the human spirit and letting it fly (Virgin)
8. To provide the best customer service possible (Zappos)
9. Helping customers enhance and maintain their biggest asset (Lowe's)
10. A relentless ally for the individual investor (Charles Schwab)
11. Improving health and well-being around the world (Merck)
12. To organize the world's information and make it universally accessible and useful (Google)
13. We make background checks better (sample for background check company)
14. Helping select the right candidates faster and cheaper (sample for background check company)
15. Connecting people (sample for Slack)

We recommend a two-round process for refining purpose and behaviors, starting with executives and then moving down to other employees (figure 6.1). For example, begin with a draft by the CEO, then share it with the broader organization for input. Make edits, then share it one more time

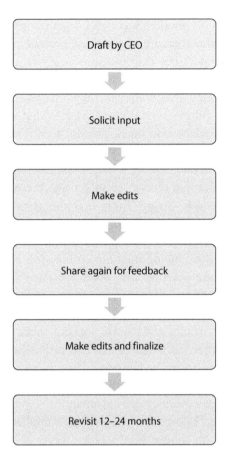

Figure 6.1
Process to determine mission/purpose and behaviors/values

for feedback before finalizing. Everyone should have an opportunity to voice their thoughts, especially for the behavior statements, but iterative group editing is inefficient. Most important, revisit your statements every twelve to twenty-four months or whenever a major change to the leadership team, the size of the organization, or a geographic expansion occurs.

Basic 3: Know who you (and your company) are

One of the more dangerous errors of many high-growth organizations is to overreach in their emulation of other successful companies. For a startup leader to be aware of another successful organization, that organization already has had some measure of sustained success in reaching a greater scale than the founder's current organization. Given that cultures change with organizations, there is almost always a temporal mismatch between what a leader is seeing at aspirational companies and what founders *need to see* about their culture several years prior to that stage. After all, was Google's intensive talent assessment process a driver of their success or was it really their search algorithm? Was Netflix's success due to their infamous culture, or did they achieve it *despite* the environment they created? Not so long ago, many leaders tried to act like the role models profiled in Jim Collins's *Good to Great*.[11] Today it is almost ridiculous to think of mirroring the old management practices of previously "great" companies such as Wells Fargo, Circuit City, and Fannie Mae.

Leaders run the risk of sending unintended mixed messages by implementing a "best practice" they borrowed from another company or the latest *Harvard Business Review* article. Understand your context, and make a conscious decision about whether someone else's program makes sense in your desired culture. If you are not sure, think twice. Many alleged best practices are often just bright, shiny objects that distract your and your employees' attention from the behaviors that are vital to the culture you want to build. Every practice will affect your culture, but understanding how it will is often an overlooked assessment.

Our advice to "know who you are" also applies to the leadership teams of high-growth companies. There will never be another Reed Hastings, Tony Hsieh, Katrina Lake, or Elon Musk. You can learn from successful leaders, but inspiration and useful tools can be drawn from many sources. We encourage you to apply the best practices for your context while understanding your specific skills and biases. A strong self-awareness brings clarity and flexibility when dealing with dynamic and complex management situations.[12] Authenticity also endears leaders to their team, with research confirming positive links between authentic leadership and others' engagement, satisfaction, commitment, and trust in the leader (among other outcomes).[13]

Basic 4: Align programs to support your desired culture

Many startups embark on well-intended and often intensely time-consuming efforts to articulate a compelling set of statements about their organization's

Table 6.2
Identifying program alignment with desired culture exercise

Purpose	Values	
We make renting easy	Drive to succeed	
	Open communication	
	Efficiency	
	Team/family spirit	

Ante	Aligned	Against
Market-level compensation and health benefits	Flexible time off policy (team/family spirit)	Confidential questions at all-hands (open communication)
Job descriptions	Merit-based pay for performance (drive to succeed)	Food budget >2% of total wages (efficiency)
Company-provided laptop and devices	Activities and events budget ~2% of total wages (team/family spirit)	
Moderate remote work flexibility	Company wiki and open Slack channels (efficiency)	
	Quarterly engagement survey (open communication)	

desired culture (e.g., mission, vision, values, purpose, etc.). However, even slightly aspirational aspects of those ideals will be heavily outweighed by the actions of the organization's leaders. If leaders' actions are counter to the desired culture, cynicism and mistrust will follow. Therefore, understand what message your existing programs, policies, and performance management processes are broadcasting, and adjust those systems to better align with your desired culture.[14]

Table 6.2 provides a simple exercise to help you identify any potential misalignment between your programs and your company's purpose or values. Think about your programs and processes in three categories: ante, aligned, and against. An "ante" is a program, policy, or benefit offering that is a core and common offering across most employers (it is your "pay to play" fee). Examples of an ante might be direct deposit of paychecks or company-provided laptops. A program is "aligned" if it directly supports your organizational purpose and values. Examples of aligned programs for a company in the education and learning space might include extensive training opportunities, tuition reimbursement, or time off to volunteer in a classroom. Finally, a program is "against" if it has the potential to create an employee perception that contradicts your organizational purpose or values. For example, the cofounder and former CEO of Cleo, a high-flying startup with goals of "making a better workplace for parents" through its parenting benefits platform, eliminated a work from home policy and shared her frustration that employees were not working enough hours.[15] Programs and practices in the "against" category should be adjusted or removed with haste.

Basic 5: Ensure good two-way communication with your team

In the absence of information, your employees will fill that void with rumor and speculation, and news spreads faster and more widely when it is false.[16] In a startup environment already characterized by uncertainty, it is especially critical to maintain constant communication with your team. Although the specific content will be unique to your organization, you can intentionally structure the communication cascade within your organization using an existing framework (see table 6.3). You can also repeat the same message to reach your team from different sources across different venues to better ensure that they internalize the message.[17]

Communications are critical in organizations because they affect employees' trust.[18] We have found this point to be especially relevant in startups that have recently increased their number of management layers. Many startup leaders will attempt to step up the frequency of their personal communications by hosting roundtables, setting up skip-level meetings, and so on. Although well-intentioned, relying solely on centralized, leader-directed communications is a near impossible practice to effectively scale. As layers grow, you need a communications framework that also

Table 6.3
Sample communication/meeting framework

Frequency	Duration	Topic/Purpose	Attendees
Quarterly	1–2 days	Offsite planning	Leadership team
Monthly	1–2 hours	Business review	Leadership team
Biweekly/monthly	30–60 minutes	All hands	All workers
Weekly/biweekly	30–60 minutes	Staff meeting	Each manager with their team
Weekly/biweekly	30–60 minutes	One-on-ones	Each manager with each direct report

relies on and supports the agency of middle management in disseminating company messages.

An effective communications framework will emphasize *fewer messages, more often, from more sources.* If repetition stimulates both awareness and credibility, a smaller number of messages communicated more frequently will have greater impact than the laundry list of CEO-delivered messages that many leaders present. Moreover, leaders often grow tired of saying the same things over and over, which may explain their tendency to undercommunicate vital issues that have yet to sink in with employees. Do not fool yourself, though. It can take a long time for some messages to connect with employees, and even longer if you are trying to reshape preexisting perceptions. Thus diversifying message sources can help sustain the energy behind the message and help employees understand it from multiple viewpoints.

Beyond top-down outbound communications, a good communication framework also has channels that enable the flow of bottom-up information. Bottom-up feedback is vital for providing course correction information, identifying "hot spots" of employee dissatisfaction (often because a manager is in over his or her head), and heading off dangerous rumor mill fodder.

Gathering useful bottom-up information typically requires more than a classic suggestion box solution. We recommend three primary methods to stimulate employee feedback. The first is through a regularly reoccurring meeting cadence in which team members at all levels are asked (and expected) to raise questions and concerns publicly. If those questions are addressed clearly and confidently, and the person who raised the question is celebrated instead of scorned, similar questions will flow freely in the future.[19] This is an excellent tactic that can be built in to almost all other types of meetings.

The second method for gathering feedback is through one-on-ones between a manager and an individual employee. These provide opportunities for two-way feedback to clarify priorities and share information. If managers are not hosting one-on-ones with their team members *at least* every month, they are probably missing rich opportunities to gather information that can be used to improve the company's processes or the employee's experience. Organizational leaders should publicly share their expectation that all managers conduct regular one-on-ones and should provide basic content suggestions (e.g., sample questions, topics) to help inexperienced managers make the most of the experience (see the following list). We also encourage managers to keep ongoing notes from their discussions in Google Docs or another online platform for accountability purposes.

SAMPLE ONE-ON-ONE TOPICS

- What has gone well since our last conversation?
- What has not gone as well as we would have liked since our last conversation?
- What are the current top priorities?
- What do you need help with?
- What questions do you have?

The third method to stimulate feedback and gauge employee sentiment is through employee surveys. Surveys are currently in vogue, and a multitude of online platforms (e.g., CultureAmp, TinyPulse) allow convenient slicing and dicing of the data. Given the rapid change experienced by most fast-growing organizations, we recommend using a brief survey to gather employee input and measure change over time two to four times per year. This frequency has several benefits, including encouraging you to keep the survey short and your follow-up actions focused. Figure 6.2 provides an employee survey life-cycle chart.

Before committing to an employee survey, be mindful that a poorly managed survey has the potential to be counterproductive.[20] The following tips can help you avoid common mistakes and get the most out of your survey efforts.

First, ask the right questions. As a starting point, consider the Gallup Q12, which offers some of the most commonly researched questions in the employee engagement space.[21] Also know that the structure or topic of a question can dramatically influence the score (e.g., a typical average favorability score for "I am proud to work for XYZ company" is likely to be much higher than "I believe my total compensation is fair"). What you learn really depends on what you ask!

Second, try to figure out what "good" looks like. Changes in scores over time and differences by geography, department, leader, or demographic *within your workplace* are incredibly valuable because they clearly illustrate trends and differences. But how will you know if you really have a problem? Obtaining a relevant and relative comparison illuminates how your organization truly stacks up.

Third, make sure you take action with the employee feedback collected through a survey. Some organizations hand it off to the HR department, basically forgetting about it. Others find themselves in analysis paralysis. Still others share the results and promise to work on a laundry list of

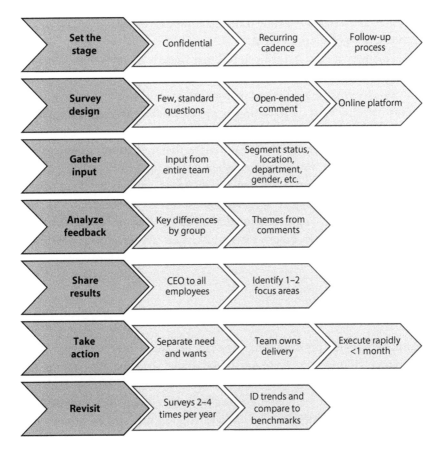

Figure 6.2
High-level employee engagement survey and action planning process

items, but they never make any meaningful progress. These *in*actions can have dire consequences. Some data indicate that as many as 29 percent of employees think surveys are useless, and around 80 percent do not believe their manager would follow up on the results of a survey. Sadly, they had good reason for these beliefs; 27 percent of managers surveyed did not even bother to read the results, and more than 50 percent of managers said they viewed results but took no action.[22] Sentiments like these kill employees' willingness to respond on future surveys, and over just a couple of iterations, this pattern will render surveys utterly worthless and ultimately cost you one of your main lines of bottom-up communication. You cannot take every employee rating or comment at face value, but you do need to be prepared to change *something* if the data indicate problems or substantive opportunities for improvement.

Finally, a survey can tell you whether there is a problem and perhaps where (i.e., in what group) the problem resides. However, it will not tell you exactly what that problem is in most cases. Before you react, engage in further discovery efforts with members of affected teams. Also consider the context around the survey. There are natural periods of change and upheaval within high-growth organizations that may affect responses. One common example we see occurs when a new round of funding precipitates the hiring of several new department heads who quickly if not bluntly assess their teams, change what and how work gets done, and jockey for position among each other. Some of these issues may be figurative bumps in the road, whereas others are more serious and require intervention. Survey data are a useful tool for leaders, not a substitute for them.

Conclusion

Although many organizations brag about exotic practices that boost employee culture (and these often take center stage on popular business websites and magazines), startups should be wary of buying into new fads. Building and maintaining a healthy culture is a lot like building and maintaining a healthy physical lifestyle: A good diet and exercise require constant activity but can get boring, just as good communications and management practices require constant upkeep but lack flair. To build a great culture for your company, embrace the idea that your culture will inevitably evolve as you grow (and that's okay!), understand what makes your company unique, and align your programs and practices in ways that affirm the desired culture. Establishing and utilizing rich two-way communication between management and employees will help you evaluate your current culture and will provide opportunities to strengthen it in the future.

7

Performance Management and Goal Setting

Clarity, Consistency, and Consequences

We were once asked by a large, well-regarded international technology company to conduct return on investment (ROI) analyses of their various HR programs. We worked with the relevant managers, execs, and internal customers to set out the costs and the monetized outcomes (desired and actual) of programs for hiring, training, incentives, etc. When working with them on performance management, the group was consistent in the desired outcome: improved performance to be achieved through employee engagement, appropriate distribution of rewards, addressing performance problems, etc.

When, later, we assessed actual outcomes of the program, there was near-consensus as well: productivity decline; disengagement of managers and their reports; "rewards" that were resented by high and low performers alike; an increase in legal liability when faced with the positive reviews given poor performers; and so forth. Needless to say, the question of ROI in this case—at least the valence—was straightforward. The return on investment of their performance management program was substantially negative.

I wish I could report that this was an anomaly. My experience elsewhere is often the same. Performance management may be the Achilles heel of HR, a practice that seems like such a good idea—but, as executed, is often more damaging than not. Gallup found that only one in five employees strongly agreed that their company's performance management motivated them to do outstanding work; only one in six strongly agreed that their performance reviews inspire them to improve their work.[1] This painful reality is reflected in the revolving door of faddish programs intended to "fix" performance management. Ratings (3, 5, 100 points?), forced rankings, rank-n-yank, eliminating ratings, MBOs, OKRs, and so on.

Ironically, the real answer may be to go back to the basics: clear, impactful goals; timely, effective feedback; and aligned, meaningful consequences. Then execute those with minimum bureaucracy and maximum manager-employee engagement and collaboration.

—STEVE MCELFRESH, PHD, FOUNDER OF HR FUTURES, FORMER CHRO OF NEW RELIC AND DUO SECURITY, AND PRESIDENT AND CEO OF SARATOGA INSTITUTE

CHAPTER 7 RUNDOWN

The Problem
With growth, frontline workers and middle management are further removed from the most important priorities. They need clarity and direction.

The Plan
Clarify priorities and create mechanisms for reinforcing them with your people.

The Basics
1. Set simple and clear goals.
2. Provide effective feedback.
3. Create consequences that matter.

The Problem

Your startup is investing deeply in the selection and attraction of talented employees, and your leaders are spending a meaningful percentage of their time and funding to reward, develop, and engage those workers. Yet growth has caused your founders to get further away from the frontlines, and consequently, they struggle to provide meaningful direction around key priorities. It is frustrating that the link between your company's efforts to engage and motivate employees is not translating into more organizational success.

In addition to basic business requirements such as product-market fit and appropriate capitalization, effective goal setting and performance management processes are critical to achieving (realistic) desired results. Unfortunately, founders, managers, and employees tend to have a strong negative association with performance management practices because the term tends to convey that an "issue" needs to be fixed. It is not surprising that some startups avoid performance management altogether and instead lavish praise on everyone, hoping, often through some magic, that things will just work out (they rarely do). Other startups try to do something, but ultimately view their performance management options as a choice between two evils: treating workers as disposable (rapid terminations with little documentation that result in legal and cultural risks) or using administratively onerous and disingenuous performance improvement plans to address problems.

Based on our experience, founding teams commonly take a rapid action approach until employee sentiment deteriorates or the first lawsuit appears; then they take a major swing toward overengineered and bureaucratic performance improvement plans that are mostly designed to avoid litigation risks. Predictably, managers resist the latter, exclaiming that "we don't have time for this!"—and they are right. A growing startup does not have time for overly bureaucratic processes that exasperate managers, reduce employee trust, and promote adversarial relationships with highly skilled workers.

A handful of startups avoid the predictable swings from rapid action to overwrought bureaucracy by adopting objective and key results (OKR) processes that take an upstream approach to clarifying goals and expectations in advance. Unfortunately, although the intent is sound, the execution usually is not. OKR practices are overwhelmingly broken in the startup community; they typically leave management teams feeling administratively overworked and workers exposed to leaders' whims. Effective performance management is, without question, a major challenge for startups.

The Plan

A fundamental problem when implementing an effective performance management program is that individuals and entire organizations typically have a shortsighted view of what the concept entails. Before diving in, let's first establish a more complete picture. Professors Angelo DeNisi (Tulane) and Kevin Murphy (Limerick) describe performance management as

> the wide variety of activities, policies, procedures, and interventions designed to help employees to improve their performance. These programs begin with performance appraisals but also include feedback, goal setting, and training, as well as reward systems. Therefore, performance management systems begin with performance appraisal as a jumping-off point, and then focus on improving individual performance in a way that is consistent with strategic goals and with the ultimate goal of improving firm performance.[2]

Many startup leaders feel overwhelmed by the prospect of implementing a comprehensive performance management program, and *we get it*. Most do not have any formal HR training and have incredibly limited time and bandwidth. A few simple methods can help these startup leaders align employees around goals and deal constructively with performance issues. A solid performance management program can usually be traced to three major elements: clarity, feedback, and consequences. When these three elements are aligned and effectively applied, the employee-manager relationship is strengthened, trust is enhanced, and wasteful administrative tasks are minimized. The critical outcome is that the employees you have invested so much time and money into attracting and retaining are supported and developed rather than discarded.

Clarity is the product of communicating a focused list of consistent and reasonable expectations. Many high-growth startups are challenged by the focus and consistency required for clarity—it always feels like there is simply too much to do. However, if you do not figure out how to concentrate your and your employees' efforts on the most critical activities, the organization becomes mired in a swamp of initiatives competing for attention. To quote Karen Martin, author of *The Outstanding Organization*, "when everything is a priority, nothing is a priority."[3]

Another threat to clarity at startups is rapid change, which makes goal setting trickier than it is in more stable organizations. Distilling what matters for your employees requires a thoughtful exercise in creating clear goals for the organization, various teams, and individuals that match a reasonable time horizon.

Performance management is not just about deciding who stays, who gets fired, and who gets a raise. It is about guiding your entire workforce toward better performance. Rather than discussing goals only once at an all-hands meeting and then saving them for an annual review, goals need to be communicated frequently and in detail with teams and individuals so they can meaningfully coordinate action. Managers should be holding regular one-on-ones with each employee to discuss goals and progress toward those goals, meaningfully acknowledging the context in which each employee operates. One-on-ones are the foundation of most communication in growing startups; they provide powerful opportunities for course correction and other performance management information (unforeseen consequences of a managerial initiative, need for goal revision, etc.).

To reinforce goals and feedback, real consequences need to be tied to employees' varying levels of performance. If a team or an individual has a big win, you want to encourage continued striving for success and for others in the organization to emulate their success. Rewards and recognitions, both meaningful consequences, are powerful signals in that regard.[4] If you fall into the common trap of praising everyone and making only surface-level distinctions between top and bottom performers, your message gets muddied and the feedback conveyed lacks teeth. When it comes to performance management, equality and equity are rarely the same. The consequences you offer are an acknowledgment of previous work but also the spark for future work. Table 7.1 demonstrates a variety of performance management approaches.

Winning organizations value a two-way employment relationship, understanding that the actions (or inactions) of management influence employee effort and trust. Managers provide goal clarity, share regular performance feedback, and deliver differentiated consequences. The investment in employees is too large and the reputational impact is too great to treat workers as disposable. We expand on these ideas that will help you build an effective performance management methodology in the three basics: clarity, feedback, and consequences.

Table 7.1
Performance management approaches

Rapid Action	Performance Improvement Plans (PIPs)	Goldilocks Zone
Limited performance feedback before involuntary terminations	Extensive documentation required before termination, but workers are often surprised by PIPs	Provide frequent, lightly documented feedback regarding performance versus expectations, encouraging constant course corrections
Typically provide severance packages to mitigate legal risk	Less legal risk, therefore fewer severance packages; workers often given a choice between PIP or severance, creating the (often accurate) perception that PIPs are being used for risk mitigation rather than authentic improvement tools	Less legal risk, therefore fewer severance packages— no formal PIPs necessary if ongoing one-on-ones are well-documented
Major cultural risks—fear of being terminated without warning	Moderate cultural risks—PIPs viewed as fait accompli and are therefore disingenuous	Minimum cultural risks related to involuntary terminations if managers are legitimately supporting workers and providing constructive feedback
Leadership perceived as capricious when poorly communicated departures happen quickly (workers viewed as disposable, sowing anxiety)	Leadership perceived as weak and insincere for using a slow and administratively onerous program to make changes	Leadership viewed as both supportive and decisive

The Basics

Basic 1: Set simple and clear goals

Management scholars recognize that effective goal setting is one of the most robust predictors of performance outcomes an organization can implement.[5] It is not surprising that goals have also found their way into startup practice. Yet as startups scale, they tend to oscillate wildly and inefficiently between too little and too much goal setting. This is an understandable pendulum swing as leadership teams identify and attempt to address ever-changing issues. Most startups typically go through several failed cycles before settling into a process that works. Of course, about the time they find a process that works, the situation changes, and they are forced to do something else to survive the next crisis! For this reason, we do not recommend a one-size-fits-all solution for goal-setting programs but instead advocate for *just enough* structure to provide clarity for team alignment.

How much is "just enough"? For most startups, the market, team, and even the product change so rapidly that granular, long-term goals become exercises in futility. However, if you go too big picture, employees cannot use the goals to meaningfully inform their daily priorities and decisions. To help decide on a "just enough" approach, we advise leaders to consider two specific factors: organizational level and frequency. Tables 7.2 and 7.3 discuss the pros and cons of common decision points around goal setting.

For any goal-setting system to work, goals must be clear enough to understand, appropriate for the team to which they are assigned, and *stable during the measurement period*. We typically see a longer cycle at the company level and a relatively shorter cycle at the team or department level. Most organizations are best served by a two-tiered goal-setting program in which company-wide goals are set annually and team/department level

Table 7.2
Goal setting by level within an organization

Organizational Level	Positives	Negatives
Individual	• Best opportunity to tie results to objectives at an individual level (you know who is performing and who is not)	• Most work is team-based, with many aspects outside the control of any one individual • Goals and priorities tend to change more rapidly the deeper you look in an organization (individual goals are usually obsolete before they are ever documented)
Team/department	• Most major initiatives are team-based, often coordinating many people across internal boundaries	• Difficult to determine measurable results at an individual level
Company-wide	• Provides valuable big-picture direction to the organization • Supports budgeting, resourcing, and prioritization	• Does not effectively inform behaviors or assist in tracking results at an individual level

Table 7.3
Goal setting frequency/time frame

Frequency/Time Frame	Positives	Negatives
Monthly	• Most timely and responsive approach to rapidly changing environment	• A thoughtful process is nearly impossible to execute within this time frame, particularly at more granular planning levels
Quarterly	• Timely and responsive to changing environment and provides stability over time	• Process must be light and aimed at team/department levels of the organization to be effectively executed
Annually	• Minimizes the administrative burden of goal setting by infrequent planning	• Great likelihood of changes to goals and priorities during measurement period, particularly if performed for deeper layers of the organization

goals are established quarterly. Because individual-level goals can vary a great deal in terms of reasonable time-to-completion estimates, they are best evaluated on a more flexible basis. We recommend that individual goals be set and monitored through regular (documented) check-ins between workers and their direct managers.

Even if goals are set at an appropriate organizational level and on a reasonable frequency, they need to be clearly articulated to guide desired behaviors. The most commonly used tool for creating clear and actionable goals is the SMART (specific, measurable, achievable, relevant, and time bound) goal-setting approach.[6] Other frameworks tap into similar concepts.[7] We support the SMART framework generally but acknowledge that leaders may still find it challenging to define sufficiently clear goals for their employees. To guide more detailed discussions, consider walking through some variant of Patrick Lencioni's priming questions for driving clarity[8] with your team during the goal formation process:

1. Why do we exist? (Why are we in business?)
2. How do we behave? (What are our values?)
3. What do we do? (What is the core nature of our business?)
4. How will we succeed?
5. What is most important right now?
6. Who must do what?

Answers to the first three questions should be tightly maintained as decisions cascade from the organization level into teams/departments and individual goals. Diverging even modestly on these can create misaligned efforts and "us versus them" mentalities across teams, which can be fatal in startups where everyone needs to be on the same page. Answers to the next three questions (framed around the team/department or individuals) can vary depending on the unit's charge but must nevertheless reinforce the answers to the first three questions.

Before moving on from goals, we want to acknowledge the popular practice of using OKRs as an approximation of goal setting.[9] In many startups, OKRs are set at the company, department, and individual levels quarterly and are scored on a percentage basis for each goal (usually targeting 70 percent to encourage aspiration toward stretch achievements). We strongly support clearly defined goals (objectives) and specific measures to track those goal's achievements (key results), but many growing companies misuse OKRs and may be better off moving to less trendy, but more powerful goal-setting practices. OKRs rely on detailed numbers to be effective, which are not easily or meaningfully computed in most startup work (e.g., How do we "score" the output of complex, team-based knowledge work?). As a result, leaders end up relying on convenient but often immaterial or arbitrary measures of success such as completion date, completion percentage, or elements of quality, engagement, and satisfaction. Similarly, setting target performance at 70 percent of the goal is overly complicated and may create awkward dynamics (e.g., incentivizing "sand bagging" during goal setting, fostering a culture in which it is deemed "okay" to *constantly* fail). We recommend that most startups set goals and treat them like commitments.

With clear goals at appropriate organizational planning levels and frequency, you are placing yourself on an excellent path to improving and ensuring the performance of your teams. Examples of quarterly goals tied to job type and department are shown in table 7.4.

Basic 2: Provide effective feedback

Providing effective feedback seems intuitive, but it is a common failure point in many performance management programs. Organizations and leaders may spend countless hours setting goals and communicating them to the company, but then they inexplicably avoid providing actionable input to teams before the measurement period is completed. How does this happen

Table 7.4
Sample quarterly goals by job type or by department

Inside Sales Account Executive:
1. New revenue $
2. New accounts #
3. Customer satisfaction net promoter score (NPS) of X+
4. Being a good team member (subjective: teamwork, communications, etc.)

Software Engineer:
1. Story points completed
2. Code and documentation quality
3. Being a good team member (subjective: teamwork, communications, etc.)

Recruiting team:
1. X+ positions filled per recruiting team member (on average) for the quarter
2. Hiring manager NPS of X+ on thirty-day posthire survey
3. Employment branding built out on [job sites] by [date]
4. Being a good team member (subjective: teamwork, communications, etc.)

---

to otherwise smart people? Perhaps this failure is related to overwrought goal-setting processes that create performance management exhaustion. It is more likely to happen, however, because managers are reluctant to have difficult discussions with team members whose work is not aligned with expectations. Indeed, our experience suggests that many managers fear demotivating their employees when delivering anything other than positive feedback (in their defense, classic research indicates that almost a third of feedback interventions end up with poor results).[10] Whatever the reason, in the absence of feedback, skilled employees are not given a chance to correct their course, and the entire organization suffers.

An annual or semiannual performance review process is the most common remedy for addressing manager feedback avoidance. Through an anniversary-based or focal point review process, companies ensure that every employee receives written feedback (often accompanied by a rating) about his or her performance. However, this regular review practice has eroded somewhat as many organizations eliminate or significantly pare down performance ratings in an attempt to avoid potential negative side effects.[11] Although formal reviews are flawed in many ways (often emphasizing accountability over improvement), *not* having them can create even more problems![12] If workers do not receive clear and direct feedback, they are unlikely to know whether they are doing well or not (performance) or whether they are working on the right things at the right times (priorities). Research indicates that ambiguity and uncertainty about how one's efforts are contributing to performance are linked to negative employee outcomes such as dissatisfaction, psychological strain, and intentions to quit.[13] Taken together, we recommend that organizations provide some sort of periodic formal review, even if it is primarily as a "jumping-off point"[14] for richer feedback efforts.

An overarching criticism of typical performance reviews is that they try to accomplish too much: provide information, guide improvements, justify raise and promotion decisions (or firings, on the flip side), and provide a legal safety net, just to name a few.[15] To overcome this problem, organizations should provide performance feedback to individuals and teams more frequently and with a more pronounced focus on development (versus just assigning a score for pay raises). One way to facilitate this process is to make sure managers and their employees are having regular one-on-one meetings every two weeks for about an hour each (with other less formal check-ins on an "as needed" basis). Many managers in a startup environment are relatively new and may not have quality one-on-one meeting experience from which to draw. Moreover, many will still feel like individual contributors and may balk at devoting so much time to each subordinate. But it is imperative that these managers invest honestly in the process and avoid cancelling meetings or cutting them short.[16] As former Intel CEO Andy Grove once noted, "the subordinate must feel that there is enough time to broach and get into thorny issues."[17] We also recommend an agenda for one-on-ones to help managers and subordinates overcome tendencies to avoid awkward and difficult discussion points over more tactical, but less critical topics.

Effective one-on-one agendas vary, but one approach we endorse is for managers and employees to use starter questions to initiate discussion. These questions push both parties to discuss the most substantive issues but also provide latitude for employees to deviate. We also advise managers to assume that most of the meeting content is "owned" by the subordinate rather than taking a top-down approach. Here are five questions managers can use to initiate a one-on-one with employees across a broad range of experience, levels, and functional areas:

1. What went well since our last check-in?
2. What could have gone better since our last check-in?
3. What do you need help with?
4. What else is on your mind?
5. How do you think you're doing versus expectations?

Even if your organization sets a clear expectation that one-on-ones occur regularly and provides the starting point for what those discussions should look like, you must still "inspect what you expect." There are some very good technology tools to support one-on-ones (e.g., GetLighthouse, Lattice), but a lower tech (and almost equally effective, in our experience) option is simply using a shared Google Doc or similar format. The virtue of using a support tool for one-on-ones is twofold: It provides an inexpensive and flexible method to keep track of commitments, and it is visible to relevant stakeholders.

Under the shared doc approach, a manager creates the document and then shares editing access with the employee, the manager's manager, and their internal HR contact. Repeating standardized questions across meetings (to allow changes to become visible), encouraging employees to provide responses beforehand to ensure prior thought, and reminding both parties of team goals and the individual's development plan (usually at the top of the document) are helpful methods for guiding and keeping tabs on the process. During or shortly after each one-on-one, the manager and the employee can take notes on activities, achievements, expectations, and course corrections in the shared document. An example of this format is depicted in the following list.

ONE-ON-ONE TEMPLATE (MANAGER COMMENTS DURING OR
AFTER THE MEETING ARE IN ITALICS)

[Worker Name] / [Manager Name] One-on-One

INDIVIDUAL DEVELOPMENT PLAN (LEAVE AT TOP OF
ONE-ON-ONE DOCUMENT)

1. Focus areas:
   a. Learn more about and practice how to close candidates
   b. Learn more about and practice how to talk about equity with candidates
   c. Build skills in identifying best sources to generate qualified and interested candidates
2. What I need my manager's support on:
   a. One-on-one learning sessions and practice

TEAM GOALS FOR THIS QUARTER (LEAVE AT TOP OF
ONE-ON-ONE DOCUMENT)

1. Eight or more positions filled per recruiting team member (on average) for the quarter

2. Hiring manager net promoter score (NPS) of ten-plus on thirty-day posthire survey
3. Employment branding built out on LinkedIn, Indeed, Facebook, and Glassdoor

[MOST RECENT DISCUSSION DATE]

1. What went well since our last check-in?
    a. New recruiting manager started work, and we have rebalanced workloads.
    b. *I agree. This was a pain point in the past, and I'm excited to bring the extra resource in.*
2. What could have gone better since our last check-in?
    a. Onboarding took quite a bit of my time, and we still need to clarify some responsibilities.
    b. *That's fair. Let's firm up team responsibilities by the end of next week. Should give the new recruiting manager an opportunity to weigh in as well.*
3. What do you need help with?
    a. Clarify responsibilities within the recruiting team and the new structure.
    b. Making progress on my development plan—I haven't set up learning sessions because I feel like I've been too busy.
    c. *Okay. Deadline for responsibilities clarification is end of next week, which I'll take the lead on and ask for everyone's input before finalizing.*
    d. *Before our next one-on-one, please schedule one, 1-hour learning session for the two of us to work together each of the next four months.*
4. What else is on your mind?
    a. Will we continue to have one-on-ones now that a recruiting manager is in place? How can I ensure this new hire will accelerate versus limit my career growth and skill development?
    b. *Yes, let's continue biweekly one-on-ones—at least for now. If we decide they're not needed, we can change the frequency or cancel. Let's continue to have candid discussions about your career aspirations and development progress.*
5. How do you think you're doing versus expectations?
    a. I think I'm doing well. Thanks for the help resetting the expectations of my hiring managers.
    b. *Yes, you are doing well. Let's get a working session on your development plan on the calendar for next week.*

[PRIOR DISCUSSION DATE]

1. What went well since our last check-in?
   a. Offer out to new recruiting manager—great skills and good fit with the team.
   b. Should help to balance workloads. The team is pretty stretched.
   c. *I agree. Let's get the job requisitions transitioned by the end of next week.*
2. What could have gone better since our last check-in?
   a. Getting behind on company-wide recruiting activities as we have been interviewing recruiting manager candidates and figuring out how to reallocate responsibilities.
   b. *How have your clients responded to your discussions with them about this short-term priority shift, until we get the new hire in place?*
3. What do you need help with?
   a. Air cover with hiring managers and department heads as we get a new resource in place. Should help in the long term but is creating some pain in the short term.
   b. *You've got it. I'll send a note to all your clients later today, with a CC to you.*
4. What else is on your mind?
   a. I don't want my hiring manager clients to be disappointed in me. I'm feeling like I'm letting them down by focusing on internal activities (like selecting a new recruiting manager and sorting out responsibilities).
   b. *Do you think a note from me to your clients will address this concern, or can I do more to support you with this?*
5. How do you think you're doing versus expectations?
   a. I feel like I'm letting my internal clients down while doing what I'm being asked to do for our functional team.
   b. *You're doing great—just communicate what's happening to your hiring managers, focusing on the mid- and long-term benefits of adding a new member to our team. I have no concerns with your progress or priorities.*

The manager of the manager or a human resources professional should review one-on-one notes periodically to ensure the discussions are happening at the desired cadence and are getting to an appropriate level of depth and candor. If not, there is a coaching opportunity to improve the quality of the one-on-one for the manager. Likewise, having records allows higher-level or HR managers to evaluate supervisors' concerns about the performance of a worker. Did the manager do her or his job properly? Have the manager's expectations been made clear during one-on-ones? In summary, solid one-on-ones can dramatically reduce the need for cumbersome and condescending performance improvement plans and create meaningful dialogue that delays the need for time-consuming and administratively complex processes such as 360-degree feedback (which may become more viable later in the startup's life cycle). When time, energy, and other resources are limited, investing in one-on-ones as a supplement to formal feedback processes produces the best return on investment (ROI) we have found for most startups.

Basic 3: Create consequences that matter

Appropriately aligned consequences can drive the overall performance of a group upward over time. Misaligned consequences do the opposite. A surprising number of managers have convinced themselves—sometimes with the help of still nascent and very much developing neuroscience research[18]—that they should recognize everyone equally and abundantly. This is a risky approach.

Most people want to perform well at their jobs and want to be recognized and rewarded for performing at a high level.[19] In most groups, there is usually some degree of acceptable variance in performance, and rewards and recognition should also vary to keep performance trending upward. Recent data collected by PayScale shows that top-performing organizations are more likely than lower-performing organizations to rely on merit or pay-for-performance incentives to keep top performers engaged and on board.[20] When done transparently and fairly, reward and recognition differentiation can help lower performers by creating a clear incentive to improve (i.e., more rewards) and highlighting role models (i.e., top performers) they can emulate.[21]

The core reasons to provide differentiated consequences are to draw attention back to organizational goals and to reinforce feedback. Even in startups that promote a relatively strong culture of providing direct feedback, some managers are still prone to avoid or dilute the tough stuff. Likewise, employees make all sorts of attributions to deflect and resist critical information. When meaningful consequences are attached—whether they involve raises, bonuses, promotions, an expanded role, or even thoughtful social recognition—messages are heard more clearly. Therefore, managers should make a habit of discussing wins as well as losses, offer public recognition for successes and require after-action reviews for all major initiatives, and ensure that remedial efforts (such as training or mentoring) are tied to openly discussed skill or knowledge gaps. The closer these actions are linked, the better the connection between pay, promotion, and performance.

We typically focus on the direct effects of consequences on employee reactions, but it is also important to know that there can be indirect consequences. Employees are constantly observing the performance management efforts of the organization, especially as it relates to their most proximal coworkers, and they draw conclusions about which behaviors are welcomed or unwelcomed. To promote a culture of fairness, we advocate for a reasonable level of transparency. We are not suggesting you share all details of every termination or promotion (indeed, research does suggest some potential downsides to transparency), but other workers should see causes and effects.[22] Does repeatedly exceeding sales quota result in a promotion, or is it more valuable to participate on cross-functional project teams? Will organizing team happy hours lead to positive consequences, or does that person risk being viewed as more social than serious? Do people depart from the company with little explanation, or do you have team discussions when there is a misalignment of priorities or a gap in required skills? The point here is again reinforcement. If you can help your team understand what actions and behaviors lead to what outcomes (and those outcomes are meaningful), they are much more likely to perform the desired behaviors.

You will inevitably face skeptics and resistance to a pay-for-performance program. Rest assured that it is possible, in fact, to implement such a plan without creating a ruthless, cutthroat culture. As noted previously, most top performing organizations follow some variant of this approach and do not rely on notorious "rank and yank" or even forced distribution schemes. After deciding to move forward with a pay-for-performance program, many organizational leaders jump quickly to nuanced technical questions: "Should we have three ratings or five?" "What should we call those rating categories?" "How many percentage points of merit increase should be tied to each rating?" These questions will be relevant for your organization eventually, but they are not as important as doing the homework around goal clarity and regular feedback mechanisms. Nail the basics and you will have much more latitude with the technical details.

Criteria may vary	Methodology may vary	What should not vary
• Performance • Potential • Market rates • Position within range • Tenure • Skills	• 9-Block • Ratings and weightings • Forced vs. recommended distribution • Various forms of calibrations	• Clear criteria for determining pay changes • Well-defined processes for budget allocation and approvals

Figure 7.1
Link pay to performance

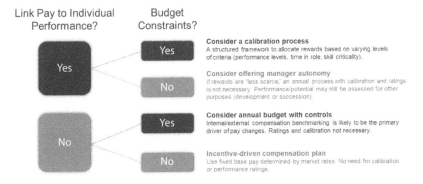

Figure 7.2
Compensation process decision tree

There are many ways to link pay to performance, but it takes intentional design thinking to do it well. Figure 7.1 shows how those elements could be linked, although your organization may exhibit differences based on its culture, needs, and language. There is no such thing as "one size fits all." Figure 7.2 shows a compensation process decision tree (based on budget constraints and a desire to tie pay to performance), and table 7.5 describes "traditional" performance management, today's popular agile performance management, and our view of modern performance management to help kick-start your thinking.

Table 7.5
Modern performance management is a middle ground (Goldilocks zone)

Traditional Performance Management	Modern Performance Management	Agile Performance Management
Senior leadership sets high-level goals.	Goals are set at several levels (company, division, department, team, individual).	Individuals set their own goals.
Expectations are not usually effectively cascaded to all major roles, resulting in confusion and internal conflicts.	Clear expectations are documented and well-aligned across the organization for all major roles.	Fluid expectations often serve as an excuse for failing to identify and document any goals.
Goals are set and reviewed annually.	Goals are set and reviewed on multiple cycles (month, quarter, year).	Goals are set and reviewed continuously with no formal reviews or calibrations.
Review is primarily backward-looking (prior performance).	Review is backward- and forward-looking.	Reviews are primarily forward-looking (developmental).
Documented feedback generally occurs only at the time of annual review or discipline.	Frequent documented feedback and coaching is expected on multiple cycles (month, quarter, year).	Informal feedback and coaching are expected frequently (at least monthly) and often from multiple sources.
Limited ongoing administration outside the intensive annual review process.	Moderate ongoing administration with a less extensive focal point process.	Extensive ongoing administration to do this effectively—often poorly executed.
Corrective action is progressive discipline or formal written warnings.	Regularly documented one-on-one performance feedback eliminates written warnings.	Performance issues are often not well-documented.
Superficially strong pay for performance due to subjective annual ratings.	Multiple criteria drive pay decisions, usually involving thorough calibrations.	Weaker pay/performance tie—usually either subjective or driven by the market.

Conclusion

Many founders think of performance management as something very personal and unique to their culture. This is true. It is also true, however, that decades of management research support many of the key concepts we have advanced in this chapter. Most startups have very little chance of pulling off a sophisticated "do it all" performance management system, but if you can master the basics of establishing clear goals across levels and time frames, providing meaningful and frequent feedback, and tying impactful consequences to performance variations in your organization, you can build a powerful program that propels future growth.

8

Legal and Compliance

Common Traps and Easy Answers

As employers grow, they face materially increased litigation risk. Therefore, they need to start mitigating that risk early in the growth trajectory—usually at the fifty to one hundred employee threshold. There are several key areas where even moderate early efforts can significantly mitigate employment litigation risk before the employer becomes a bigger target. Some of the most common issues we see involve arbitration agreements, wage-hour compliance, and leave of absence/disability accommodations. There are many other things for employers to review in this phase of their growth trajectory, of course, but taking action in these core areas can significantly reduce litigation exposure and is well worth the effort.

—ERIC STEINERT, PARTNER, EMPLOYMENT LAW PRACTICE,
SEYFARTH SHAW LLP

CHAPTER 8 RUNDOWN

The Problem
More growth equals more litigation risk.

The Plan
Find an employment lawyer and protect yourself against the most common
   legal and compliance issues.

The Basics
1. Standardize most employment practices.
2. Establish compliant wage-hour policies and practices.
3. Set up compliant accommodation policies.

The Problem

Most startup leaders want to treat their workers well and to uphold legal standards. But employment law is complex and dynamic, and it is often difficult to quickly distill for leaders who do not possess legal training. Given everything else happening inside a startup, legal and compliance processes often take a back seat. Indeed, it is extremely rare for a startup to consider legal and compliance efforts as a core activity unless there is a strong connection to that business's product, service, or customer base. Consequently, many business leaders tend to think of legal and compliance topics as necessary evils *if they think of them at all.*

Legal and compliance processes have not experienced much technology disruption or employer investment recently, which contributes to leaders' inattention to this aspect of their people operation. Unfortunately, legal issues can swell quickly and become highly disruptive when a startup reaches critical mass. Without taking a (multiyear) break to go to law school or bringing in a team of prohibitively expensive in-house counsel, what is a growing startup to do?

The Plan

Several reasonable steps can be taken by startups to avoid disastrous litigation stemming from noncompliance issues. Most startup leaders do not need to be legal experts, but they should plan to engage one early to prioritize common trouble spots and get in front of them by creating compliant, scalable practices in those areas. We are not lawyers, and our writing is intended only to provide you with an idea of common issues; this discussion does not serve as a substitute for a good lawyer (so find a good lawyer!). A good employment lawyer with national experience can help you normalize practices across all fifty states (as well as address some international arrangements), put your wage-hour practices in order, establish compliant leave and disability accommodations, and set up arbitration agreements and insurance policies that protect your company from the worst outcomes. With some leg work up front, you can minimize the time, money, and reputational costs that befall so many startups.

The Basics

Basic 1: Normalize your employment practices across all fifty states

You may have only one location today and no immediate plans to grow beyond headquarters, but you should still create policies that can move cleanly across state lines. Interstate employment arrangements happen surprisingly fast and tend to catch startup leaders off guard. For example, your company may need to find a critically talented person with a unique skill set who is not readily available or affordable in the home labor market. Then, out of nowhere, you are introduced to the perfect person— and that person lives somewhere else. This person may even be willing to travel but not to outright relocate to your home state. Sometimes valued employees you do not want to lose will move away but express a willingness to continue working remotely. Thus you can go from a local employer to a national employer overnight. If your policies and practices do not hold up in another jurisdiction, you may be looking at significant trouble down the line.

To get ahead of this problem, create policies and practices that meet *at least* the minimum legal thresholds across all fifty states from the start. To do this effectively and efficiently, you will need to develop a relationship with a law firm that has a national employment practice. In many cases, taking a national approach will mean offering slightly more generous terms or worker protections than the minimum standard required by law in a given location, but it can also translate into saving countless hours and errors by allowing your company to offer exactly the same terms and conditions to all of your U.S.-based employees. To the extent possible, stick with a single approach to policies and agreements and make exceptions only with adequate knowledge of the likely trade-offs. Local variations that lead to individual-level negotiations and one-off deals may sow confusion and mistrust in your ranks.[1]

As you strive to normalize legal forms and documents across states, plan to have your lawyer review each of the following annually:

- Employee handbook template
- Employment offer letter
- Employment agreement (used selectively, usually for only a few executives)
- Consulting services agreement
- Independent contractor agreement
- Nondisclosure agreement
- Arbitration agreement template
- Inventions, intellectual property, and proprietary information agreement
- Employee separation agreement
- Equity plan document

Templates for most of these documents can be obtained inexpensively from Legal Zoom or from your local Small Business Development Council, but most high-growth startups will benefit greatly by spending extra to work with a good employment lawyer. A good lawyer will help you navigate specific situations and develop clearer, more generalizable documents (e.g., employee handbook, preemployment package documents) that can greatly reduce misunderstandings and conflicts.[2]

Basic 2: Establish compliant wage-hour policies and practices

When a startup reaches about fifty employees, when their product/service achieves significant name recognition, or when the company receives publicity related to a new round of funding, the risks associated with noncompliance on essential employment elements become especially pronounced. Some important mandates are relatively straightforward to address (e.g., sexual harassment prevention training in some states[3]), but others are vastly more nuanced. Issues are particularly pronounced in the area of wage-hour practices. Given the extraordinary complexity of wage-hour requirements, we advise having an employment counsel complete a full audit of wage-hour policies and practices, including the following:

- Exempt/nonexempt classifications
- Independent contractor status
- Meal and rest periods

- Wage statement/payroll records
- Incentive/commission plans
- Timekeeping/overtime/off-the-clock work

Primarily for simplicity's sake, startups often choose to pay all their workers a salary with no overtime compensation (treating them as "exempt" status). This decision not only makes some administration easier but is validated by knowledge workers saying they would feel demeaned to be treated as hourly workers who are required to rigidly track their work time, meal periods, and other breaks. This practice, however, can introduce unexpected problems. Workers who may be improperly classified as nonexempt have enormous leverage if they experience any type of adverse action (e.g., termination).

To illustrate some of the pitfalls, consider a common wage-hour claim scenario in California. In this context, a potentially incorrectly classified employee's leverage is created largely by the fact that even if an employer loses just one element of a multipart claim, the employer is responsible for the employee's legal fees as stipulated in the Private Attorneys General Act,[4] and this can become the largest expense by far. In fact, well-meaning but inattentive employers could easily find themselves liable for more than four times the annual pay of a given employee by failing to classify overtime eligibility properly. The following example details a representative single-employee exemption status claim:

- A computer software employee earns $80,000 and is treated as salaried exempt (as of January 1, 2020, the minimum annual rate of pay that exempts computer software employees from California overtime provisions is $96,968.33[5]). The employer and employee maintain sick and vacation time records but do not track meal periods, breaks, or daily start and stop times.
- After a little more than two years of employment, the employee is terminated for poor performance (statute of limitations is typically two years).
- The employee claims to have been misclassified for pay purposes and should have been nonexempt (discrimination and harassment complaints often accompany these claims).
- The employee further claims being required to work through lunch regularly, and breaks were not provided. The employee estimates this work at an average of ten hours of overtime per week over the period.

- Potential back pay of $124,800.
  - Overtime $62,400 (hourly rate $40 × 1.5 overtime rate × 10 hours per week × 104 weeks)
  - Meal period $31,200 ($40 × 1.5 × 5 × 104)
  - Rest period $31,200 ($40 × 1.5 × 5 × 104)
- Potential liquidated damages of an additional $125,000 (double the back pay award).
- Plaintiff's legal fees of $50,000+ (often $600+/hour) to reach mediation or $250,000+ to try the case.
- Defendant's legal fees of $50,000+ to reach mediation or $250,000+ to try the case.
- Additional potential statutory penalties, waiting time penalties, and itemized wage statement penalties.

The employer bears the responsibility to classify workers properly and to keep accurate time records, and workers cannot waive their rights through acceptance of an offer letter. If the employer has not kept records of time, the employee can essentially make any assertion related to time worked, and the burden of proof shifts to the employer. In the current example, even if the employer contests the claim and eventually wins outright in court, the defense lawyers will still need to be paid (possibly hundreds of thousands of dollars). When resources matter, that is a particularly steep price to pay.

Even if your company is particularly well-funded, the leadership team is unlikely to welcome the distraction involved in defending a lawsuit. Furthermore, severance offerings of several weeks or even several months are unlikely to have much of a mitigating effect on these types of claims. If a realistic complaint is made, the best course is usually to settle it as quickly as possible. Wage-hour claims are often a no-win proposition, and we strongly recommend working with a legal or human resources professional to evaluate the exemption status of all the positions at your company. If you insist on tackling this yourself, check the U.S. Department of Labor Wage and Hour Division website[6] as well as your state's labor policies.[7] If there is any doubt about the status of a role, the best policy is to treat those workers as nonexempt.

Another common wage-hour claim relates to independent contractor status. Core issues that distinguish an employee from an independent contractor include, but are not limited to, the nature of control your organization has over the provider's work, how integral the provider's work is to your organization, the relative permanency of the relationship, and various financial components of the work. Independent contractors can be appealing to a resource-strapped organization because the company avoids dealing with payroll taxes, overtime and minimum wage requirements, Social Security, Workers' Compensation Insurance, unemployment and disability insurance, and various other compliance issues mandated by wage and hour laws. Employers often do not even track the time of workers treated as independent contractors. As you might imagine, if a worker who has been treated as an independent contractor is aggrieved or feels mislabeled, the employer has significant potential liability for all of the wage-hour issues mentioned here as well as additional state and federal tax concerns.[8]

Unfortunately, determining whether a worker is an independent contractor or an employee can be a long and surprisingly complicated endeavor, typically involving numerous government agencies.[9] Speaking to the complicated nature of contractor status inquiries, U.S. courts have not established a single rule for making determinations and have argued that any determinations must be made based on "economic reality" versus other technicalities (in other words, there is lots of gray area).[10] The Department of Labor Standards Enforcement starts from the position that a worker is an employee until proved otherwise. As with overtime eligibility, the employer bears responsibility for classifying workers correctly and cannot use an offer letter or consulting agreement acceptance letter to waive employee rights.

Given these risks, utilizing "gig workers" or other contracted workers in your growing company should come with some measure of protection for the organization. Many organizations use a third-party "employer of record" (EOR) to support these types of workers. In an EOR relationship, the worker performs work for your company while another organization serves as the official employer and is directly responsible for taxes, benefits, unemployment, and various compliances. Many well-known companies provide EOR services, including TriNet, ZeroChaos, Velocity Global, Target CW, and Nexus CW. By contracting with an EOR to employ independent contractors on your behalf, those workers will not receive the same benefits, perks, and programs as your regular employees. Instead, those workers receive benefits provided by the EOR (usually lower-cost minimums required by statute). This relationship does, however, tend to be slightly more costly than directly employing an individual. Typically, all costs are passed through with a 3–5 percent markup, and it will take some meaningful time and effort initially to set up the EOR relationship. That said, once you have a provider in place, it is relatively easy to onboard contractors on an ongoing basis.

When an established organization is considering employing a one-off independent contractor or consultant, we recommend working with an employment lawyer or an HR professional to evaluate each situation. *If in doubt or if you do not have the time or the resources to do the analysis, we generally recommend that you treat most workers as employees.* When you encounter individual gig workers who insist on working as independent contractors, you can accommodate them by setting them up through an EOR. If that arrangement does not work for the gig worker, it is time to find a different worker.

Basic 3: Set up compliant accommodation policies for leaves of absence and disabilities

Establishing and following compliant leave of absence and disability practices can be surprisingly challenging, especially in employee-friendly jurisdictions. Indeed, the complex overlay of state and federal laws regarding protected leaves of absence and disability accommodation presents many opportunities for unintentional deficiencies. Most major employment law firms can provide advice on compliant employee handbook policies and can support the education of HR staff and managers, but addressing complicated real-life situations can be challenging.

One common scenario involves a poor performer who goes out on a leave shortly before being disciplined or terminated. Too often, startups have a dangerous mix of inadequate documentation of the performance problem and policies written or implemented in noncompliant ways. When this happens, expensive litigation ensues, wherein the employee claims the termination/discipline was based on the leave or disability and not on the actual performance issues. If an employer cannot establish a justifiable defense (through documentation), a costly settlement may be the least expensive way out.

To hedge against this possibility, we recommend consulting with an experienced HR professional or employment counsel prior to taking an adverse action (discipline, demotion, termination, etc.) against any employee who requests a leave of absence or may have grounds to assert a disability. The advice given is usually to improve the documentation of historical performance issues and to suspend any adverse action until the individual returns to work and continues to exhibit performance shortfalls. Although this is not ideal and incredibly frustrating, your organization will be spared an expensive settlement, avoid potential reputational damage, and have a talking point for encouraging managers to take their performance management duties and communication seriously.[11]

Basic 4: Implement arbitration agreements and obtain employment practices liability insurance

Although creating and implementing compliant practices from the start is the obvious goal, you can take other steps to protect your company. One such technique is to use arbitration agreements. Eric Steinert, an employment lawyer, notes that "arbitration is a faster, cheaper, and fairer way to resolve employment disputes. They reduce litigation volume because plaintiffs' lawyers are less likely to take on cases that lack jury potential." Arbitration agreements are not a substitute for treating your employees fairly and can be tricky to implement in some states (e.g., California), but they are worth the effort.

Employment practices liability insurance (EPLI) also provides some measure of protection, typically covering claims related to sexual harassment, wrongful termination, discrimination, retaliation, failure to promote, defamation or libel, invasion of privacy, emotional distress, and employment-related breach of contract (such as making promises and representations to potential employees that turn out to be untrue). EPLI can be a low-cost method to backstop the risks associated with becoming a larger and higher-profile employer, particularly if you have staff in high-risk areas (for key statistics on EPLI, see table 8.1). Bundled with coverage, some carriers offer

Table 8.1
Employment practice liability statistics

Of companies with fewer than one hundred employees, 23 percent invest in employment practices liability insurance coverage.

During FY2019, 80,806 charges of employee discrimination were resolved by the Equal Employment Opportunity Commission.

More than 40 percent of lawsuits related to employment practices liability insurance are filed against private companies with fewer than one hundred employees.

U.S. companies have a 10.5 percent chance of having an employment charge filed against them.

California employers have a 46 percent higher chance of litigation than the national average.

It takes 318 days for the average employment claim to be resolved.

The average cost for cases that result in both defense and settlement payments is $160,000.

The median for employers with less than $25M revenue is a $5,000/year premium with $10,000 deductible for $1,000,000 in coverage.

Sources: https://www.hiscox.com/documents/2017-Hiscox-Guide-to-Employee-Lawsuits.pdf; https://www.eeoc.gov/statistics/all-statutes-charges-filed-eeoc-fy-1997-fy-2019; https://www .advisenltd.com/data/epli-loss-data/; https://www.nkytribune.com/2019/02/keven-moore-all -companies-can-get-sued-cost-of-not-having-employment-practices-liability-insurance/; https:// amtrustfinancial.com/blog/insurance-products/top-trends-employment-practices-liability-claims.

"free" templates and examples of handbooks and policy documents that can increase your compliance. If you are confident in the compliance of your policies and procedures, you can reasonably consider taking a higher EPLI deductible to keep your costs down. If you are uncertain, start with a lower deductible while you work on shoring up your policies and procedures.

Conclusion

You face serious legal risks as your startup grows and becomes more visible. In fact, it is typically a question of *when*, rather than *if*, an issue occurs. Many leaders of high-growth companies fancy themselves as pirates (rather than Navy captains) until they experience significant (and potentially disastrous) legal consequences. Most often, these issues center around failing to adhere to basic mandates across state lines, wage-hour policies, and leave of absence and disability policies. Investing proactively in legal and compliance solutions can save much pain later. If your policies are deficient (or if you are just unsure), reach out to an employment law firm immediately. A good firm will help you get your house in order and be able to point you toward other protections (arbitration agreements and insurance options). If a reasonable claim is made against your company, wrap it up as quickly as possible. Employment law generally favors employees over employers, and it will almost certainly be more costly and time consuming to contest a claim (even if you win). In summary, do not shirk on the basics; even modest investments in legal and compliance efforts early on can save you significant monetary, time, and reputational resources down the line.

9

How and When to Construct Your People Team

Supporting Your Scale-Up

More companies should take the time to be as strategic about their people team as they are with the rest of the organization. I see many companies waiting until things are broken to bring in a "real" people leader, rather than being proactive about it from the start. Growing companies wait until they have problems including high employee turnover, low employee morale, missed recruiting goals, and an inability to attract senior talent before thinking strategically about the function. The first practice companies can employ is to hire a strategic people leader before they think they actually need one. Second, they need to staff the function properly with the right number of individuals rather than running it too lean. Third, companies need to have their people leader as a member of the executive team, fully integrated with, and a true equal to, the other functional leaders.

—SAYDEAH HOWARD, CHIEF TALENT OFFICER, IVP

During the last eighteen months at Airbnb, we have grown from about 3,500 employees to more than 6,500 employees, plus another 3,000+ contingent workers. Early on, most high-growth organizations are almost solely focused on building the product and growing the team. A subset of growing the team is selecting and growing good leaders. Later, specialty areas start to develop within the people function, such as compensation and benefits, learning and development, and employee programs. Operations and compliance are often last. While these areas can be band-aided early on, they become a major need if you're approaching one thousand employees and continuing to scale rapidly. In fact, operations becomes mission critical to ongoing growth. You just can't attract talent fast enough or retain talent well enough if you don't have your house in order—and it's a lot easier to put some foundational pieces in place long before you get to one thousand employees than it is to rework the employee experience when you're that size and doubling every year.

—QUASAR HAMIRANI, GLOBAL HEAD OF PEOPLE
OPERATIONS AT AIRBNB

CHAPTER 8 RUNDOWN

The Problem
You can see that people matters matter, but you're not sure how or when to build a people (HR) team to handle them.

The Plan
Understand the key landmarks that indicate when and how the people function should change.

The Basics
1. Zero to twenty employees, or the "DIY and outside help" stage.
2. Twenty to one hundred employees, or the "Bring in the pros" stage.
3. One hundred to four hundred or more employees, or the "Scale-up" stage.

The Problem

As you grow, things get complicated. Your investors start pushing for action, and technology vendors begin swarming with promises to solve all your people management problems. You must do something, but you do not know what. You think you are ready to bring in a recruiter and maybe an HR/people person, but how do you know what to look for? What should you even expect a full-time HR person to do? Should you start with an entry-level person to push the paper or jump to a VP-level person to build the strategy? When do you build out a people team even further?

A frequent topic that comes up in our consulting work is how and when a company should build an HR team. There are a near-infinite number of HR service delivery models in play across the startup landscape, making it difficult for an inexperienced leader to know which is best for his or her company. Some organizations invest in dedicated support during their seed stage, whereas others wait until they are well-funded (Series B and beyond) before bringing expertise in-house. Timing questions aside, the current demand for good "people professionals" is so high that even finding someone has become difficult. In fact, a major search firm recently told us that there were so many active VP people/chief people officer/head of people searches going on for startups in the San Francisco Bay area that they were turning down a greater number of lucrative search contracts than they were accepting. Moreover, in some niches, the average compensation for chief people officers has even surpassed the market rate of CFOs.[1]

The Plan

A major challenge for executing a successful people playbook is knowing *when* to apply which practices. There is no substitute for experience, but thankfully there is a vast network of potential advisors to tap into and some general rules of thumb you can use to guide your approach. We walk you through some of the basics in this chapter.

When determining how to build your HR organization (including recruitment), you need to periodically map out the current and upcoming needs of your organization. We hope earlier chapters have helped shed some light in that area, but remember that you can refine your plan and avoid costly mistakes by seeking advice from experts. In your company's earliest stages, most of that expertise will come from external consultants and advisors, but over time you will begin insourcing expertise.

If you have secured venture capital funding, one of your early resources will be your VC's talent partner (TP).[2] TP expertise varies but is usually weighted toward deep executive search backgrounds with limited, but still valuable, insight into designing compensation programs and referring key vendors. If you do not have a strong TP connection, or if you are not receiving the level of engagement you want from your TP (some TPs support one hundred-plus portfolio companies and are stretched too thin), you can and should find expertise in other ways. Many prior CHROs and VPs of HR now provide a broad range of consulting/advice to startups (our firm, Series B Consulting, is one such firm) and can be contracted on a retainer basis to help only when you need them. This is often less expensive and smarter than trying to prematurely hire a CHRO or VP of HR. Most venture-capital backed companies will not need a chief HR/people officer until after their Series C funding. They demand a hefty salary and will not be able to fully deploy their skills until the organization grows to a critical mass (usually beyond one hundred employees).

In addition to seeking expert advice during your periodic planning activities, you should also involve all of your functional teams. Department heads should play especially critical roles during planning, answering questions about how they plan to develop the team, what the triggers to add resources should be, and how their approach integrates with other teams. Integration is essential for successful scaling. If engineering gets too far ahead of product or if sales falls behind marketing, disasters ensue. Early on, CEOs should be deeply engaged in resource planning (staff/vendor/contractor) to ensure reasonable growth sequences and to help coordinate between internal teams. As the company progresses, a COO or CFO may take the lead. Eventually, a strong VP of HR or CHRO will be needed to manage the process and navigate complex integration challenges, utilizing a more mature HR team in plan execution.

Like the rest of your organization, the structure of your people team will evolve over time. The basics advanced in this chapter focus on understanding which HR services are most important and how those services should be fulfilled at key headcount thresholds.

The Basics

Basic 1: One to twenty employees, or the "DIY and outside help" stage

Until an organization reaches about twenty employees with plans to grow significantly beyond that, they should *not* employ a dedicated HR professional. At under twenty employees, the founder/CEO (and probably their executive assistant) will be responsible for payroll, recruitment, benefits, compliance, culture, communications, performance management, training, etc. This can feel like a lot, but things do not need to be too complicated at this point. The initial HR focus of early-stage startups should be on delivering reliable payroll, essential benefits, and basic recruiting initiatives. In this stage, a startup probably should not be running sophisticated learning and development programs, creating career ladders, or articulating cultural principles.

We typically recommend that startups engage a professional employer organization (PEO) once they have as few as three to five people on staff. A PEO consolidates payroll, benefits, compliance, and several other services (see chapter 4). In the area of payroll and benefits administration, whether working with a PEO or a payroll provider plus benefit broker (described next), you are looking for a solution that meets your needs for at least the next few years because there are tremendous financial and operational costs when making changes. When choosing a PEO, try to avoid getting talked into a hot new technology solution backed by a mutual investor or an obscure solution with low pilot pricing. These are basic administrative services that are not going to be differentiators for your organization—unless they do not work (i.e., the wrong kind of differentiation). We suggest sticking with tried and true brands and fully featured solutions to confidently carry your company to one hundred or more employees.

If you are uncomfortable with a PEO, payroll service providers can provide a reasonable alternative. Payroll service providers will help you not only pay employees on schedule but also manage payroll taxes and appropriate tax forms. As your organization grows more complex, a provider can be expanded to track and manage type of pay, withholdings, performance bonuses, leave and paid time off, COBRA processing, and numerous other benefit deductions/contributions (e.g., retirement, health insurance). Dozens of payroll providers offer free trials and multiple pricing and service packages: Intuit Quickbooks, ADP, Gusto, Paychex, Square Payroll, OnPay, Paycor, PrimePay, Zenefits, and Rippling. Small businesses can expect to pay a base cost of $30 to $50 per month in addition to a small ($3 to $10 per employee) fee.

When selecting a payroll provider, consider pairing them with a benefits broker to help you construct an appropriate benefits package for your team. Most payroll services offer other HR technology add-ons for an upcharge, including recruitment or onboarding support. Many of these add-ons will sound neat and promising, but are not truly value-adding early on. However, that may change once your company is bigger and more complex. Even if you do not enroll in the add-ons right away, you should at least consider whether a provider has high-quality offerings when making your initial choice. Similar to our point about PEOs, changing service providers

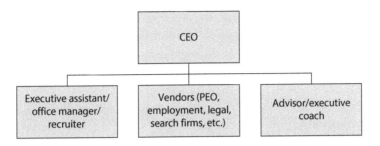

Figure 9.1
HR organization required (<20 employees)

down the road can be extremely disruptive. Finally, you tend to get what you pay for with service providers, so do some due diligence rather than simply choosing the lowest-cost option.

Beyond administering pay and benefits, recruiting is a critical HR function you will need to fulfill. Early on, your team will most likely be constructed from founders' first-, second-, and third-degree professional and personal networks. Investors may also actively support your recruitment and networking efforts. With fewer than twenty employees (figure 9.1), you generally do not need to hire a recruiter or HR professional. Everyone on the existing team should be helping to build the team in some way: getting to know people in the space, sharing the vision of their growing company with those people, framing roles and responsibilities, participating on interview panels, and onboarding new hires. Every hire requiring the investment of precious equity or cash should be deeply and uniquely vetted by the founders because roles are extremely fluid during the period of development and discovery. Finally, do not dedicate excessive time or resources toward building formal recruitment programs or acquiring technology tools in this phase. These programs usually only add value at higher levels of recruiting velocity (twenty-plus hires per year).

Basic 2: Twenty to one hundred employees, or the "Bring in the pros" stage

The first nonfounder leaders are typically hired at around twenty employees, with another wave arriving at around fifty employees. The creation of a middle management layer is an important organization-altering event for startups. Most middle managers will deeply want to contribute to the founders' vision and, as a result, seek clear and constant direction from the top. This manifests in a barrage of questions about processes and policies that usually do not yet exist at the organization, including but not limited to the following:

- Can we launch a training program that the engineering team is requesting?
- Should we approve tuition reimbursement for someone's certification exam?
- What does it take to get a promotion?
- What is our policy about working remotely?
- What are the expectations for email/Slack/text response time and standard work hours?

The questions go on and on. This period in a company's life cycle is usually difficult for the founding team because they have been able to "wing it" and take ownership on so many previous decisions. Maintaining their previous approach after adding multiple layers of management, however, is irresponsible if not outright impossible. Successful leaders must learn how to set direction and delegate decisions to experts. In this spirit, hiring the first full-time HR professional is appropriate at twenty to fifty employees.

The aim of the first HR hire should be to help bring order to some of the organization's newfound chaos and help leadership think through questions of policy and process. Carmela Krantz, founder of Woven HR, says, "Recruiters and HR people are not interchangeable. Strategic HR leaders are incredibly valuable throughout a startup's growth. Hire a size-appropriate head of HR/people operations early, setting the foundation for how an organization prioritizes its employees—around fifty people or earlier."

The first HR professional should typically be brought in at a director or senior director level (i.e., people operations director [POD]) as shown in figure 9.2, serve as a member of the leadership team, and focus largely on helping your company document and deliver basic policies and processes (e.g., an employee handbook, new hire onboarding, and exit processes). The POD should be capable of completing many core tasks independently but will often be coordinating with specialist vendors. We generally recommend that startups at this stage target a strong, experienced HR generalist (ten or more years of experience) with a broad set of skills across the HR function. The person you hire for this role will probably not be the person you need as a VP or CHRO at a later stage, so it is important to discuss the

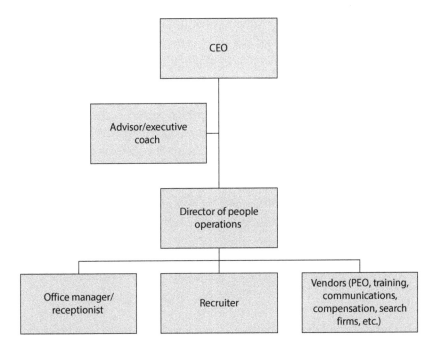

Figure 9.2
HR organization required (~50 employees)

prospect of being layered in addition to selling the company's growth story to candidates.

Your new HR leader will be tasked with building a fledgling HR team, usually made up primarily of recruiters. We suggest hiring your first internal recruiter sometime after twenty employees or whenever your company expects to hire twenty or more employees over the next twelve months. You should plan to add an additional recruiter to the team with every twenty to forty hires per year increase after that. If you do not build some in-house recruiting expertise, you will be forced to lean too heavily on external search firms, which come with significant monetary and coordination costs.

At twenty to one hundred employees, your PEO arrangement will be in its sweet spot, efficiently providing payroll, benefits, compliance, record-keeping, and some employee relations support. At this stage, you can begin considering a variety of technology tools to support employee surveys, performance management, or collaboration. Be mindful that vendors are persistent, proactive, and often overstate[3] (and some will outright fabricate) claims that their software will make your business better.[4] To avoid a proliferation of costly and distracting HR technology tools, wait until you have a material problem that can be effectively addressed by a new tool before purchasing and implementing something. We further suggest referencing academic research (when available) and independent analysts who do not take compensation for promoting software products. We particularly value Gartner's Magic Quadrant,[5] which segments the market based on providers' "ability to execute" and "completeness of vision."[6] Once you have a short list of prospective tools, get recommendations from your network, obtain demos (using a scorecard to evaluate offerings), and solicit proposals before making the leap. To reduce the need to make a platform change in the foreseeable future and avoid layering too many tools on top of one another, try to select tools that can scale with your business.

Basic 3: One hundred to four hundred or more employees, or the "Scale-up" stage

At around one hundred employees, startups with continued high headcount growth (>50 percent) should start thinking about hiring a highly experienced VP of HR or CHRO to build out a more complete HR infrastructure. A VP's or CHRO's primary charges will be to bring in a head of talent acquisition, transition the company away from a PEO, and start insourcing an increasing array of specialized work that had previously been supported by vendors. As the organization increases in complexity, more reliable and more scalable employee services become essential to success (figures 9.3 and 9.4).

When looking for a potential VP or CHRO, search vigorously for an experienced candidate. You may be tempted to stretch your first HR hire (e.g., the POD we discussed previously) into the role, but prior experience at the head of a function in a scale-up is irreplaceable—this is not a position for "learning on the fly." Your existing POD can usually be layered as a direct report under the new leader and will remain a key employee, especially during the transition. Keeping that in mind, be sure to bring the POD into discussions about potential VP or CHRO hires. The best-case scenario is that by involving the POD in the search and selection process, the POD becomes invested in and excited to learn from the new leader.

You will need to bring in a strong talent acquisition head (often a senior director level, sometimes VP) to lead your recruiting team once you start planning to hire more than one hundred employees per year, including attrition (another common benchmark is after Series C funding). Although it may seem easiest to promote a high-performing individual contributor

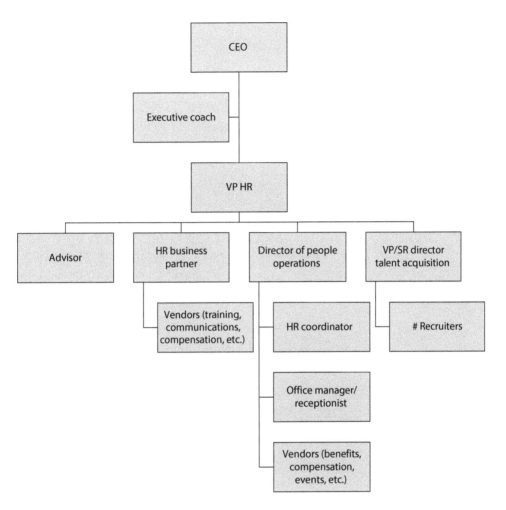

Figure 9.3
HR organization required (~150 employees)

recruiter who has been with you for a while, it is best to invest in someone with prior experience scaling a recruiting team. You want a candidate with broad experience driving efficiency throughout the recruitment and selection process, building an employer brand, integrating your company culture into the candidate experience, motivating hiring managers, coaching recruiters, and managing high-priced (and often high-ego/high-intensity) search firms. A VC talent partner's network may be especially helpful during your search. There has been a trend among rapidly growing companies to have the head of talent acquisition report directly to the CEO (acting as

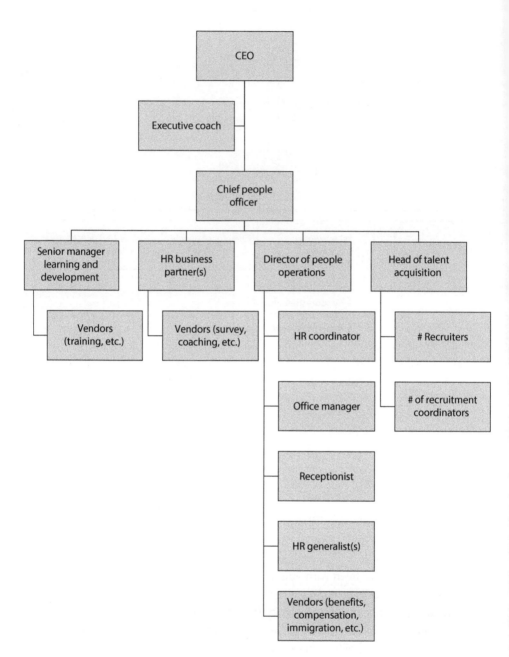

Figure 9.4
HR organization required (~300 employees)

a peer to the VP or CHRO), but we discourage this approach because the candidate and employee experience are closely linked and benefit from an integrated approach. A related concern is that CEOs often prefer to be near the action of talent acquisition, but they generally lack the skills and experience to effectively lead the operation better than a strong CHRO.

Some organizations consider outsourcing to grow more rapidly and develop their recruitment capabilities. Using the capacity and resources of a vendor can be an incredible accelerator, but it comes with additional cost and some loss of control. You will save recruiter time and candidate sourcing time, but ultimately you will pay for it with increased selection times (selection activities will fall almost exclusively to your internal hiring managers and interview teams). Moving from highly personalized cofounder-led "friends and family" recruitment to using a sourcing vendor can be shocking, especially when the vendor's team does not sit in your offices and hardly knows the organization. Furthermore, vendors typically charge 100 percent markups on recruiter time or placement fees of 10–20 percent of a candidate's first year compensation. We generally recommend building your own talent acquisition team at this stage, but recruitment process outsourcing vendors may be a necessary alternative if your company is prioritizing rapid growth and does not yet have an effective internal recruitment infrastructure in place.

In this stage, companies can benefit from transitioning off a PEO and moving many HR activities in-house. Having a strong and experienced VP or CHRO really adds value at this stage because this is a notoriously complicated process. Someone who has led this work in the past should have increased ability to see around corners, anticipate issues, and construct appropriate risk mitigation plans. During the transition away from the PEO, the HR leader will need to coordinate with technology and finance, communicate with the broader organization, select appropriate point solutions to replace employee services provided by the PEO, and build their people operations team to support the work soon to come their way.

We use the term "employee services" to capture basic employee administration needs such as changing an address, adding a dependent, ordering a replacement insurance card, modifying tax withholding, or checking the holiday calendar. Although it is ideal to provide individualized, concierge-level support for every employee service request, a somewhat less personalized but more scalable solution is appropriate for most startups. We acknowledge that this concept may be met with cynicism by founders who are trying to build a premium brand and premium experience for all customers, candidates, and workers. A more scalable solution does not necessarily equate to a poor experience, however, and on-demand self-service options are likely to be a better experience for employees than even the most caring and skilled human touch. When it comes to employee services, we have found that people tend to want answers immediately and do not like waiting in line (which is a problem if the entire team servicing requests is at a staff meeting or it is 11 p.m. on a weekend).

Beyond one hundred employees (and often up to one thousand), most organizations will have a payroll system with an integrated human resources information system (HRIS) and some insourced HR administration. At this point, most companies gain both effectiveness and efficiency advantages by building an employee self-service knowledge center (via Slack, JIRA, an HRIS landing page, or a simple company intranet) and setting up email aliases for the most common issue types (e.g., benefits@domain.com, recruiting@domain.com, payroll@domain.com, HR@domain.com). With email aliases, issues can be easily routed to service teams, even when members of those teams change over time.

Beyond one thousand employees, more sophisticated technology tools become increasingly valuable, including ticketing/tracking tools (e.g., Jira, Zendesk, Salesforce Service Cloud), more advanced HRIS (e.g., Workday), and productivity tools for employee programs and employee engagement. Economies of scale become quite pronounced past one thousand employees, and early investments can yield tremendous operational advantages. You still need to balance between getting ahead and trying to do too much too soon, and experienced CHROs will know when to move these programs forward.

As a startup shifts more markedly from founder-led to leader-led, the diverse (and often dispersed) leaders will need support in many ways. Of primary importance is understanding how the organization intends to operate and executives' expectations for the workforce. After one hundred employees, specialist HR services that were previously supported by vendors/consultants (or delayed entirely) should also move to dedicated internal teams (see table 9.1). Common services include the following:

- Compensation design, benchmarking, and leveling
- Benefits, perks, and work-life program design and communications
- Learning, training, and development
- HR operations (payroll, recordkeeping, people analytics, employee data management, employee surveys)
- HR business partnering (leader/manager coaching, change management support, employee relations, program deployment, performance management)

Table 9.1
HR resourcing by subfunction and company size

Function	0–20 Employees	20–100 Employees	100–400 Employees	400+ Employees
Payroll and Benefits	Accounting or executive assistant	PEO and HR generalist(s)	Internal HR operations staff and benefits broker	Internal HR operations staff and benefits broker
Programs	CEO and office manager	HR generalist(s) in partnership with office manager	Designed by VP of HR, executed by HR generalist	Specialized internal HR team(s): learning and development, talent management, onboarding, etc.
Policy	CEO	HR generalist in partnership with CEO	Designed by VP of HR in consultation with CEO, and administered by HR generalist	Specialized internal HR team(s)
People Strategy	CEO with support from external HR advisor	CEO consults with executive team and HR generalist, supported by external HR advisor	VP of HR in partnership with CEO, possibly supported by external HR advisor	VP of HR in partnership with CEO
Recruitment	Cofounders	Internal recruiter(s) and external search, supported by investors	Internal recruiting team supplemented by external search	Internal recruiting team with minimal external search

Table 9.2
HR focus areas by company size and stage (funding round)

Funding Round	Employee Head Count	Focus Areas
Seed/A	0–20	• Hire initial team through founder network and investor referrals. • Limited benefits, programs, and perks; focus on getting funded and establishing product/market fit. • Finance/accounting, CEO, and executive assistant combine to handle payroll and basic people management matters. • Limited to no technology support. • Obtain early advice from investor/executive coach/external advisor on how to structure and select your team. • Obtain an initial employee handbook from an employment lawyer.
A+/B/C	20–100	• About twenty employees, establish HR vendor relationships that can scale to about one hundred employees (PEO or payroll provider and benefits broker). • Hire an HR professional at twenty to fifty employees (probably manager, senior manager, director level with seven to ten years of generalist experience). Set the expectation that this person will be layered when you hire an experienced VP of HR at about 100 employees. • Hire an internal recruiter when you expect to make about twenty hires over the next year, and hire another for every twenty to forty hires after that. • Sign up for an applicant tracking system such as Greenhouse. • Start tracking and reporting core HR metrics. • This tends to be the most disruptive period of a high-growth company's life cycle. Focus on selecting an outstanding executive team and clarifying priorities and responsibilities. • Worker sentiment is likely to dip at some point during this stage. Start tracking and trending engagement. Use TinyPulse or Culture Amp, and work to address key themes. • Document people programs, policies, and procedures while resisting program proliferation (stay focused on necessities).

B+/C/D+	100–400	• First VP of people should now be in place with two to four HR team members in addition to the recruitment team.
		• VP of people should decide how to resource the recruitment team, but a reasonable ratio is one recruitment team member per about thirty hires per year at this stage (include about 30 percent turnover in that calculation).
		• Alignment and prioritization across the company become a huge challenge. Emphasize communication and clarity. Work with VP of HR to help you hire excellent department heads who can scale with you (there is no substitute for previous experience). Invest in the success of people managers with dedicated training and HR business partner support.
		• Transition from PEO/HRO to internal HR and payroll support completed while retaining a third-party benefits broker.
		• Major efforts developing skilled managers of people, building HR programs and processes, and implementing a coordinated suite of technology tools (core HRIS and payroll solution) that can scale with the company.
C/D+	400+	• Specialist work within HR has shifted internally (compensation, benefits, learning/ training) reducing reliance on vendors.
		• Economies of scale in HR support should start to appear (increasing ratio of employees to HR staff, reducing average HR cost per employee).
		• Efforts continue to develop managers of people, build/refine HR programs and processes, and implement a coordinated suite of technology tools that can scale with the organization.

Our recommendations are applicable to most startups in the one hundred to four hundred employee stage, but we acknowledge that the top HR leader can divide the work in many ways. Titles may differ widely, and some organizations may emphasize certain specialist areas earlier than others. For example, if a concern is raised by the board about bonus compensation, a company may beef up their compensation resourcing and expertise early on. Likewise, if there is a strong, consistent request from employees and department heads related to training and development, an organization will prioritize investment in learning and development sooner rather than later. Thus some variance from our guidance is expected.

Conclusion

The key takeaway in this chapter is that startup leaders must align their HR function-building activities and resourcing with their company's stage, being careful not to get too far ahead or fall too far behind the curve. Filling the right roles with the right types of people at the right time is not rocket science, but it does require some critical thought and mindful execution. Early on, you can rely on outside vendors and external advisors to manage your people operations. As your company becomes more complex, you will bring more activities in-house and need a strong, empowered HR executive to guide continued growth. The thresholds and growth patterns described in this chapter (see table 9.2), along with a network of trusted advisors, will help you navigate this journey and optimize your people operations.

10

Where Next?

Startups are almost constantly in a state of change. If you are wondering where you are going next, the only confident answer we can give is "somewhere else." Your ultimate success will be determined by the confluence of your product appeal, the external market, funding availability, and, without question, how well talent is acquired and leveraged in your organization. In this book, we have advocated for a set of fundamentals that will help you implement effective people management practices, which in turn can give you a leg up on navigating all of the other challenges your company will face.

Each chapter discusses a minimum viable offering across a set of key people management concepts. Embedded in these chapters is an acknowledgment that your startup will progress through numerous difficult transitions—revolutions in the evolution[1]—that will force you to change. We encourage you to treat our work as a handbook that you can (and should) revisit during the formative periods of your company's growth. In this chapter, we provide a brief summary for when and how to revise your people management practices.

Key Events in Startup Progressions

Many factors can prompt significant transitions within a startup, but three interrelated events are especially common drivers: new capital raises, significant headcount growth, and efforts to increase process discipline.

New capital raises, aka "more money, more problems." Raising capital is a good thing, but with its benefits come new challenges. For example, a significant investment often leads to adding a new board member who comes with a high level of interest in, and new expectations for, your company.[2] Founder-investor dynamics are notoriously tricky, particularly when there are multiple cofounders and several key investors (which tends to happen as an organization grows). Employee expectations also change at funding events; namely, employees will expect increased compensation, more resources, and bigger titles as a "true-up" for their prior contributions and sacrifices. Whatever extra breathing room you get from raising more money will quickly be reallocated to people management issues if you have not properly prepared for change. Do not be caught off guard.

Headcount growth and new leaders. With new funding, startup leaders often deploy capital by hiring new people—usually lots of new people. Adding new people is incredibly disruptive and increases complexity exponentially, especially in startups that have limited infrastructure and relatively few formalized processes. As new layers of management are added to coordinate and support employees, the distance between key decision-makers and the frontline employees increases. Communication and intentional culture-building efforts are vital to maintaining trust and alignment. Expanding headcounts predictably leads to a rise of specialists in functions and departments, which will just as predictably cause stress for early generalists in the firm. You do not need to relearn the lessons encountered by so many ill-prepared startups before you—be ready and focus on what matters.

Increasing process discipline. When headcount increases, more and more processes are required to manage complexity. How will decisions be made? What are the most important priorities (e.g., key performance indicators or objectives and key results)? Who will direct the team? How will you communicate to all the right stakeholders? The public rationale for more process varies, but the impetus is usually centered around ensuring that the organization more reliably meets its goals. With these changes, you can expect resistance. Early employees (the "old guard"), some of whom have been or soon will be layered by new leaders, can feel disenfranchised by the cultural changes associated with increased process and policy discipline. Even founders often resist a departure from "the good old days." Despite these sentiments, the status quo is no longer an option. Successful startups acknowledge this challenge and navigate through the critical transition points with a thoughtful plan for managing employee actions and perceptions.

Break Points

Throughout the book we have advanced some general rules of thumb that can be used to diagnose what people practices make the most sense for an organization of a particular size. Meaningful changes tend to occur when companies reach around twenty employees, around one hundred employees (when at least two layers of management exist in most groups), and again around four hundred employees (when three or more layers of management are prevalent). With twenty employees, a team becomes too large for a founder to manage everyone directly, and hires are generally made outside the immediate circle of friends and family. At one hundred employees, at least two layers of management exist in most groups, and leaders no longer know everyone on a deep and personal level. The next break point is typically at about four hundred employees; this growth requires three or more layers of management, and communication and culture are threatened once again. Table 10.1 outlines typical change requirements as startups move through each of these three stages of organizational growth.

When Things Break, Don't Panic

Even though you understand the events and thresholds that generally precipitate a need for change, hitting a breaking point where your existing practices start to fail can induce panic.

Do not despair. First, if your management practices are breaking, your company may just be growing—focus on some of the positives and discuss changes as part of a natural maturation process of a thriving company. Second, rely on the specific focus areas we have advanced in each chapter of this book to guide your action. Although terminology and trends may change, the underlying lessons will endure. These lessons are drawn from years of our own and others' experience in startup leadership and consulting as well as rigorous management research. In addition to the specifics, remember the following priorities when faced with your next people management problem.

Have a Plan

Plans are certain to change, but a failure to plan nearly guarantees failure. This is not a popular sentiment in the startup world today. The popular

Table 10.1

"Rule of thumb" needs in focus areas for selected organizational headcounts

Focus Area	<20 Employees	~20–100 Employees	~100–400+ Employees
Organization Structure and Leadership	• Cofounders and family/friends • No more than a single layer of management	• Experienced hires and managers of people • 1–2 management layers	• Department heads at VP+ level with significant delegated authority • 2–3+ layers of management
Talent Acquisition: Recruitment and Selection	• Network of cofounders • Recruitment is a major component of cofounders' role • Lean on support of VC talent partners • Deep relationship-building process for all roles and candidates	• Single internal recruiter, supplemented by search firm(s) • Recruitment is a major component of all managers' roles • Presence on all major online job sites (LinkedIn, Indeed, Glassdoor, etc.) • VC talent partners assist with search firm and department head identification • Define your employment value proposition • Hiring decisions led by hiring manager, with oversight and involvement by cofounders (leaders pick their teams)	• Build out an internal recruitment team, with continued support from search firms • Recruitment is a major component of all managers' roles • Robust development of employment value proposition • Applicant tracking system implemented • Core metrics tracked (i.e., time to fill) • Structured interview and selection processes in place with attention to candidate experience • Department heads have hiring authority—limited cofounder involvement
Rewards	• Professional employer organization in place with 401(k) and core health insurances • Significant equity to all early employees with standard terms • Refer to market data from Option Impact	• Professional employer organization with some internal HR resources • Cash and equity benchmarking via Option Impact or Radford/Aon • No bonus program other than for salespeople • Utilize job leveling conventions of Radford/Aon	• Transition away from professional employer organization to benefits broker plus internally supported human resources information systems including payroll • Use Radford/Aon private company benchmarking data • Consider company-wide incentive plan with varying targets by level or role

(continued)

Learning and Development Programs	• Minimal, mostly informal and social	• Develop onboarding and manager training, leveraging vendors to accelerate design • Subscribe to broad-based learning platform (e.g., Udemy) • Reimburse self-directed development up to a set amount • Avoid implementation of programs that are likely to be difficult to scale	• Strong onboarding and manager training programs are in place and reliably executed • Selection training is included in manager training • Provide limited set of additional employee programs closely aligned with employment value proposition and both low cost and low administration
Culture, Engagement, and Communications	• Informal culture, typically based on close personal relationships • Hold a regular all-hands meeting (weekly or monthly)	• Welcome the transition to management by policy and process • Define purpose: Why does our organization exist? • Define values: What are our strongest and most unique behavioral traits? • Ensure good two-way communication channels exist and repeat, repeat, repeat • Ensure all managers conduct regular one-on-ones with employees	• Revisit your purpose and values • Ensure all programs and policies align with (and reinforce) desired culture • Develop a meeting/communication framework to ensure that all stakeholders are well-informed • Ensure department heads are conducting regular team meetings • Shift balance of communications from centralized to department/team • Implement employee survey and act on the feedback
Diversity and Inclusion	• Consciously appeal to a diverse employee base; homogeneous base is increasingly difficult to diversify	• Ensure recruitment, rewards, and performance management programs treat people from all walks of life fairly and reasonably • All employees participate in vendor-designed diversity and inclusion training	• Ensure diversity and inclusion issues are considered in all policies and programs • Consider recruitment outreach efforts to underrepresented groups

(continued)

Table 1O.1 *(continued)*

Focus Area	<20 Employees	~20–100 Employees	~100–400+ Employees
Performance Management	• Cofounders share company and individual expectations directly and iterate frequently	• Document clear and simple annual and quarterly goals for the company • Ensure all managers conduct regular one-on-ones and provide actionable feedback to their direct employees and record feedback in a shared Google document	• Document clear and simple annual and quarterly goals at the company and department levels • Ensure clarity, alignment, and prioritization across all segments of the organization • Ensure alignment between individual and team performance and outcomes • Consider implementation of a performance management tool (e.g, Lattice or 15five)
Legal and Compliance	• Engage with a national employment law firm to help develop your employee handbook and initial policies and forms • Ensure policies can be applied consistently across all fifty states, even though you may only be in a single location today	• Review wage-hour policies and practices, and convert many contractors to employee status and many employees from salaried to hourly • Obtain employment practices liability insurance coverage	• Set up a relationship with a third-party employer of record for contract workers • Take another look at your approach to wage-hour policies and practices
People/HR Team	• Founders lean on VC talent partners for advice • Consider taking on an equity advisor with deep experience in people and management issues • Engage with a professional employer organization	• Continue professional employer organization relationship • Hire first recruitment and "people professionals" • Start tracking basic HR metrics • Supplement manager and director-level people leader with external advisory support	• Transition away from the professional employer organization with benefits, broker support, and build out recruitment and people professional teams • Hire VP/C-level people leader • Refine HR metrics and align programs to drive improvements • Set up an employee self-service knowledge center and email aliases for support questions

blitzscaling approach, for example, emphasizes speed at the expense of cost and quality, which has led many founders to pursue reckless strategies without questioning whether the approach is appropriate.[3] No matter how many times the authors of *Blitzscaling* appropriately and thoughtfully clarify that the blitzscaling approach is suitable only in a very select set of circumstances, these qualifiers tend to be ignored by ambitious founders. If you look around, the most successful firms are beginning to pay attention to context and look for more balanced approaches. For example, even Facebook's Mark Zuckerberg now advances a relatively modest approach: "Move fast *with stable infrastructure*."[4]

Workforce planning is a key upstream activity that sets the stage for most other people and management practices. Although intimidating to new managers, it does not need to be a scary process. A solid workforce plan is driven by four questions:

- How many workers do you think you will need?
- When do you need them?
- Where will they be located?
- What work will they be doing?

When those questions are answered, even if only directionally, you can effectively think through the reporting structure of those workers; the sequence in which they will be hired; the profile of target candidates; the selection process; the employee/candidate value proposition (including compensation, equity, programs, culture, etc.); and how to optimize the productivity of those workers (performance management, incentive programs, communication, and alignment efforts).

Drive Focus and Clarity

Throughout the book, we have emphasized the mantra "master the basics." At its core, this lesson is intended to help you focus your company's limited resources (e.g., time, money) in ways that promote focus and clarity for your employees. At most startups, there is too much to be done, far too little time to do it, and often too few resources to share. Mountains of potentially useful initiatives could conceivably benefit your company *at some point*, but doing too many of them at the same time will lead to confusion and poor execution. Determine what is most important *right now* for your company. Rest assured, things change so rapidly in startups that you will have a chance to revisit your priorities often (we suggest doing this quarterly or at the events/thresholds previously described).

When attention and resources are being distributed across multiple priorities, progress typically slows at an exponential rather than a linear rate. You have a better shot at moving three things a mile than thirty things an inch. In this same spirit, beware of bright shiny objects and supposedly "magic bullet" practices. Startup leaders and their employees are constantly exposed to new, exciting information in articles, podcasts, workshops, consulting pitches, and elsewhere and will be tempted to try many, if for no other reason than fear of missing out (FOMO) or keeping up with the Joneses. Cash is critical, but time and attention are the most valuable non-renewable resources in a startup environment. The trust and confidence of employees can be a fleeting thing (especially when options start vesting!), so ruthlessly prioritize where you invest. Your product cycle iterations may be short, but employees' memories are long.

Communicate Openly and Often

Growth typically equates to an influx of newcomers and the loss of a few old-timers. This churn essentially ensures that at any given time a number of people (sometimes even a majority) will not really know what is going on. Your employees and managers need rich and frequent information to help them understand what the most important priorities are, how the organization operates, and the overarching purpose and values of the organization. You cannot assume that employees will figure things out on their own: When you share relevant strategic information, your team will feel more empowered to act in ways that contribute to the organization's purpose.[5]

Communication begets trust, and trust begets communication.[6] If you understand how someone views the world, you can better predict their behavior and responses. This is not only interpersonally comforting but also can help prevent unnecessary surprises—of which there are already plenty in startups. When priorities change or a new leader arrives or departs, make sure people know why. Communicate regularly and genuinely with your investors, employees, and other key stakeholders. If you think you are repeating yourself too much, you are probably getting close to communicating just enough. In fact, John Kotter, author and emeritus professor at Harvard Business School, argues that many leaders have a tendency to undercommunicate important information by a factor of ten![7] Likewise, if you think too many topics need to be covered in the time or space allotted, that is often a sign that your focus is drifting and that you need to reprioritize. The key communication play for startups is to set up a strong and regularly recurring two-way information flow between constituents. One of our favorite techniques is to use a grid in which communication vehicle, venue, audience, frequency, and topics are all outlined to ensure that no key parties are overlooked.

Lead Change—Don't Fight It

This is the most challenging recommendation, in large part because it is the most nuanced. How do you know when practices should change? How do you know if an early leader is no longer the right fit? Even with the key events and headcount threshold guidelines we have provided, these are not easy questions to answer, and the best solutions will depend on many contextual factors.

If time is a leader's greatest resource, a leader's greatest enemy is inaction. We frequently see leaders struggle with "analysis paralysis" or fall into a pattern of making excuses to hold onto past practices that no longer serve the future. For example, many leaders resist moving from a freewheeling small company culture toward structured policies and processes, formal delegation, and clear decision-making rules. They perceive doing this to be a fatal compromise of their identity rather than a necessary step for growth.[8] We suspect this happens primarily because leaders do not understand the problem their company faces or what they can do about it. When you do have this understanding, it becomes easier to defeat inaction.

Understanding an issue and potential action plans is particularly helpful because it enables you to separate a tactical change from an outright identity change (for you or your company). For example, adding layers of management to oversee specialized workers at a certain headcount should not be viewed as a stifling bureaucratic process that reduces organizational nimbleness. Instead, frame this as a mechanism for more quickly distilling information flow and decision-making so the organization can improve responsiveness to customers or speed to market. Although startup leaders are usually fairly open to learning about marketing, finance, or even engineering-related functions as they grow, less effort is devoted to learning about the people practices that propel growth (and, no, inspirational leadership tales are not a substitute for actual people management). By reading this book, you have given yourself a leg up on your competition, so keep moving forward!

Ask for Help When You Need It

Following our lessons will help your company continue its growth story, but you cannot resolve every tough dilemma alone. A major theme across chapters, for example, is that context is just as important as content; a tension exists between our advice not to "re-create the wheel" and to avoid "lifting and shifting" practices from one organization to your own. Striking the right balance is tough for startups, and in most cases, the best answer is somewhere in between (the Goldilocks zone). But how will you know which options work best for you? A network of advisors with a wide variety of experience can be especially helpful in sorting through these choices. Your advisor network can take many forms, with some common examples being a VC talent partner, an in-house people leader (if you are at that stage), an experienced advisor, consultants, communities of practice, and even indirect sources such as books and well-sourced internet content.[9]

We want to devote some time to talking about venture capital (VC) talent partners (TPs). VC firms traditionally sought to boost their portfolios by providing operational support concentrated on sales, marketing, or engineering. But these firms have increasingly seen their portfolio companies struggle with people management practices. Recently, VC firms have invested significantly in TPs to offer centralized support for portfolio companies. The TP role was virtually nonexistent prior to 2013, but they are now quite common in VC firms and are becoming increasingly valuable as advisors (especially for leaders without much practical management experience). Based on our experience, most TPs have particularly valuable executive search and talent acquisition experience, and they are especially helpful in constructing a strong leadership team and recruiting key talent. An increasing number of TPs are now highly competent in other HR capacities and may also be useful in building a more holistic people operations infrastructure.

In addition, the startup ecosystem in general has expanded, and the number of people who have some measure of startup experience and, by extension, the breadth of potential advisors has increased as well. As you evaluate this pool, keep in mind that their depth of experience will vary along with their willingness to share thoughtful and nuanced advice with you. Our experience suggests that the people professionals within the startup ecosystem are particularly open and willing to share. For example, we have found that professionals affiliated with People Tech Partners and Startup Experts[10] are some of the most knowledgeable, experienced, and influential people professionals in this space.

Ultimately, you must decide which advisors offer valuable advice and how to weigh their varying perspectives. As long as you are grounding guidance in your company's context and the underlying fundamentals of what you hope to address, you will at least be able to take a reasonable action. Take comfort in knowing that you do not have to get everything exactly right and that you will likely be forced to change things again as your company grows.

Conclusion

The demands you face as a startup leader will change both you and your company in unexpected and often incredibly positive ways. You will stretch yourself beyond what you thought possible, learn more about business or people than any university classroom can offer, and positively and deeply affect the lives of many others. As you progress in this journey, we hope the lessons in this book help guide your focus on the most pertinent people management practices your company should focus on given its growth stage. In an ever-changing environment, having a plan and becoming brilliant at the basics almost always prevails over a potpourri of programs.

NOTES

1. Scaling for Success

1. Marshall Goldsmith, *What Got You Here Won't Get You There: How Successful People Become Even More Successful* (New York: Hyperion, 2007).

2. Nicholas Bloom, John van Reenen, and Erik Brynjolfsson, "Good Management Predicts a Firm's Success Better than IT, R&D, or Even Employee Skills," *Harvard Business Review*, April 19, 2017, https://hbr.org/2017/04/good-management-predicts-a -firms-success-better-than-it-rd-or-even-employee-skills.

3. Alicia DeSantola and Ranjay Gulati, "Scaling: Organizing and Growth in Entrepreneurial Ventures," *Academy of Management Annals* 11, no. 2 (2017): 640–68; Sam Dumitriu, "Report: Management Matters," *The Entrepreneur's Network*, January 23, 2019, https://www.tenentrepreneurs.org/research/management-matters; Jeffrey Pfeffer, "Producing Sustainable Competitive Advantage Through the Effective Management of People," *Academy of Management Perspectives* 19, no. 4 (2005): 95–106.

4. Throughout the book, unsourced quotes are from anonymous interviews conducted during the course of research and writing the text.

5. Ranjay Gulati and Alicia DeSantola, "Start-Ups That Last," *Harvard Business Review* 94, no. 3 (March 2016): 61.

6. For more on this tendency, see Ranjay Gulati, "The Soul of a Start-Up," *Harvard Business Review* 97, no. 4 (July–August 2019): 84–92.

7. For an interesting discussion of this point, see Robert Sutton and Hayagreeva Rao, preface to *Scaling Up Excellence*, by Robert Sutton and Hayagreeva Rao (New York: Crown Business, 2014).

8. Reid Hoffman and Chris Yeh, *Blitzscaling: The Lightning-Fast Path to Building Massively Valuable Businesses* (New York: Currency, 2018); Elad Gil, *High Growth Handbook* (San Francisco: Stripe, 2018); Scott Belsky, *The Messy Middle: Finding Your Way Through the Hardest and Most Crucial Part of Any Bold Venture* (New York: Portfolio/Penguin, 2018); Rita Gunther McGrath and Ian C. MacMillan, *The Entrepreneurial Mindset: Strategies for Continuously Creating Opportunity in an Age of Uncertainty* (Boston: Harvard Business School Press, 2000); Eric Reis, *The Lean Startup: How Today's Entrepreneurs Use Continuous Innovation to Create Radically Successful Businesses* (New York: Crown, 2011); Guy Kawasaki, *The Art of the Start 2.0: The Time-Tested, Battle-Hardened Guide for Anyone Starting Anything* (New York: Portfolio/Penguin, 2015); Matt Blumberg, *Startup CEO: A Field Guide to Scaling Up Your Business*, 2nd ed. (Hoboken, NJ: Wiley, 2020).

9. Brett Anitra Gilbert, Patricia P. McDougall, and David B. Audretsch, "New Venture Growth: A Review and Extension," *Journal of Management* 32, no. 6 (2006): 926–50.

10. For an interesting discussion of and elaboration on this metaphor, see Reid Hoffman and Dara Khosrowshahi, "How Pirates Become the Navy," *Masters of Scale* (podcast), June 4, 2019, https://mastersofscale.com/dara-khosrowshahi-how-pirates-become-the-navy/.

11. Linda A. Hill and Kent Lineback, "Are You a Good Boss—or a Great One?," *Harvard Business Review* 89, no. 1–2 (January–February 2011): 131.

12. Hoffman and Yeh, *Blitzscaling*.

13. Freek Vermeulen, "A Basic Theory of Inheritance: How Bad Practice Prevails," *Strategic Management Journal* 39, no. 6 (2018): 1603–29.

14. Jeffrey Pfeffer and Robert I. Sutton, *Hard Facts, Dangerous Half-Truths, and Total Nonsense: Profiting from Evidence-based Management* (Boston: Harvard Business School Press, 2006); Sutton also tweeted confirmation of the Wild Turkey story @work_matters, July 12, 2019, https://twitter.com/work_matters/status/1017430240933474305.

15. Larry E. Greiner, "Evolution and Revolution as Organizations Grow," *Harvard Business Review* 76, no. 3 (May–June 1998): 55–64; J. Richard Hackman, *Leading Teams: Setting the Stage for Great Performances* (Boston: Harvard Business School Press, 2002); Sutton and Rao, *Scaling*.

16. Greiner, "Evolution."

17. Robin Dunbar, *How Many Friends Does One Person Need?: Dunbar's Number and Other Evolutionary Quirks* (London: Faber and Faber, 2010); Sutton and Rao, *Scaling*.

2. Organizational Structure: Designing a Framework for Growth

1. Ranjay Gulati and Alicia DeSantola, "Start-Ups That Last," *Harvard Business Review* 94, no. 3 (March 2016): 54–61.

2. Robert Sutton and Hayagreeva Rao, *Scaling Up Excellence* (New York: Crown Business, 2014).

3. Brett Anitra Gilbert, Patricia P. McDougall, and David B. Audretsch, "New Venture Growth: A Review and Extension," *Journal of Management* 32, no. 6 (2006): 926–50; Wesley D. Sine, Hitoshi Mitsuhashi, and David A. Kirsch, "Revisiting Burns and Stalker: Formal Structure and New Venture Performance in Emerging Economic Sectors," *Academy of Management Journal* 49, no. 1 (2006): 121–32.

4. Tom Burns and G. M. Stalker, *The Management of Innovation* (London: Tavistock, 1961); Jerome Katz and William B. Gartner, "Properties of Emerging Organizations," *Academy of Management Review* 13, no. 3 (1988): 429–41; Sine, Mitsuhashi, and Kirsch, "Revisiting Burns and Stalker"; Arthur L. Stinchcombe, "Social Structure and Organizations," in *Handbook of Organizations*, ed. James G. March (Chicago: Rand-McNally, 1965), 142–93.

5. James J. Chrisman, Alan Bauerschmidt, and Charles W. Hofer, "The Determinants of New Venture Performance: An Extended Model," *Entrepreneurship Theory and Practice* 23, no. 1 (1998): 20.

6. Larry E. Greiner, "Evolution and Revolution as Organizations Grow," *Harvard Business Review* 76, no. 3 (May–June 1998): 55–64; Dennis P. Slevin and Jeffrey G. Covin, "Juggling Entrepreneurial Style and Organizational Structure," *MIT Sloan Management Review* 31, no. 2 (1990): 43–53.

7. Gulati and DeSantola, "Start-Ups That Last," 56.

8. The "iron cage" phrase attributed to Max Weber has also been translated as "shell as hard as steel." We believe the point remains the same here and take no side on the most accurate translation. For those interested in diving down the rabbit hole of this issue, see Max Weber, *The Protestant Ethic and the Spirit of Capitalism*, trans. Stephen Kalberg (Los Angeles: Roxbury, 2002); Peter Baehr, "The 'Iron Cage' and the 'Shell as Hard as Steel': Parsons, Weber, and the *Stahlhartes Gehäuse* Metaphor in *The Protestant Ethic and the Spirit of Capitalism*," *History and Theory* 40, no. 2 (2001): 153–69.

9. D. Michael Abrashoff, "Retention Through Redemption," *Harvard Business Review* 79, no. 2 (2001): 136–41; L. David Marquet, *Turn the Ship Around!: A True Story of Turning Followers Into Leaders* (New York: Penguin/Portfolio, 2013).

10. Eric Schmidt, Jonathan Rosenberg, and Alan Eagle, "*Trillion Dollar Coach: The Leadership Handbook of Silicon Valley's Bill Campbell* (New York: HarperCollins, 2019), 31–33.

11. James R. Barker, "Tightening the Iron Cage: Concertive Control in Self-Managing Teams," *Administrative Science Quarterly* 38, no. 3 (1993): 408–37; William G. Ouchi, "A Conceptual Framework for the Design of Organizational Control Mechanisms," *Management Science* 25, no. 9 (1979): 833–48; William G. Ouchi, "Markets, Bureaucracies, and Clans," *Administrative Science Quarterly* 25, no. 1 (1980): 129–41.

12. Chrisman et al., "Determinants of New Venture Performance"; Jeffrey G. Covin and Dennis P. Slevin, "New Venture Strategic Posture, Structure, and Performance: An Industry Life Cycle Analysis," *Journal of Business Venturing* 5, no. 2 (1990): 123–35; David P. Lepak and Scott A. Snell, "The Human Resource Architecture: Toward a Theory of Human Capital Allocation and Development," *Academy of Management Review* 24, no. 1 (1999): 31–48.

13. Elad Gil, *High Growth Handbook* (San Francisco: Stripe, 2018).

14. Gil, *High Growth Handbook*.

15. John R. Rizzo, Robert J. House, and Sidney I. Lirtzman, "Role Conflict and Ambiguity in Complex Organizations," *Administrative Science Quarterly* 15, no. 2 (1970): 150–63.

16. Susan E. Jackson and Randall S. Schuler, "A Meta-analysis and Conceptual Critique of Research on Role Ambiguity and Role Conflict in Work Settings," *Organizational Behavior and Human Decision Processes* 36, no. 1 (1985): 16–78.

17. We recommend the following sources as starting points: Elizabeth Harrin, "A Complete Guide to RACI/RASCI Charts," February 3, 2020, https://www.girlsguidetopm .com/a-complete-guide-to-raci-rasci-charts/; Bob Kantor, "The RACI Matrix: Your Blueprint for Project Success," *CIO Magazine*, January 30, 2018, https://www.cio.com /article/2395825/project-management-how-to-design-a-successful-raci-project-plan .html; Erik Larson, "How Instagram Used RACI to Unlock High-Speed Innovation Decisions," *Forbes*, August 22, 2018, https://www.forbes.com/sites/eriklarson/2018/08/22 /how-instagram-used-raci-to-unlock-high-speed-innovation-decisions/#15bcb804515e; Georgiana Laudi, "When Lack of Clarity Is Killing Your Team's Effectiveness: RACI for Startups," *Medium*, February 11, 2018, https://medium.com/@ggiiaa/when-lack-of-clarity -is-killing-your-teams-effectiveness-raci-for-startups-5e85a5ef9931.

18. Stephen J. Sauer, "Taking the Reins: The Effects of New Leader Status and Leadership Style on Team Performance," *Journal of Applied Psychology* 96, no. 3 (2011): 574–87.

19. Gil, *High Growth Handbook*, 173.

20. Tammy D. Allen, Lillian T. Eby, Georgia T. Chao, and Talya N. Bauer, "Taking Stock of Two Relational Aspects of Organizational Life: Tracing the History and Shaping the Future of Socialization and Mentoring Research," *Journal of Applied Psychology* 102, no. 3 (2017): 324–37; Talya N. Bauer, Todd Bodner, Berrin Erdogan, Donald M. Truxillo, and Jennifer S. Tucker, "Newcomer Adjustment During Organizational Socialization: A Meta-analytic Review of Antecedents, Outcomes, and Methods," *Journal of Applied Psychology* 92, no. 3 (2007): 707–21; Talya N. Bauer and Berrin Erdogan, "Organizational Socialization Outcomes: Now and Into the Future," in *The Oxford Handbook of Organizational Socialization* (Oxford, 2012), 97–112; Alan M. Saks, Krista L. Uggerslev, and Neil E. Fassina, "Socialization Tactics and Newcomer Adjustment: A Meta-analytic Review and Test of a Model," *Journal of Vocational Behavior* 70, no. 3 (2007): 413–46.

21. Academics have long wrestled with the issue of ideal spans of control. For key points in this discussion, see Peter M. Blau, "The Hierarchy of Authority in Organizations," *American Journal of Sociology* 73, no. 4 (1968): 453–67; Jody Hoffer Gittell, "Supervisory Span, Relational Coordination and Flight Departure Performance: A Reassessment of Postbureaucracy Theory," *Organization Science* 12, no. 4 (2001): 468–83; Michael Keren and David Levhari, "The Optimum Span of Control in a Pure Hierarchy," *Management Science* 25, no. 11 (1979): 1162–72; Kenneth D. Mackenzie, "Measuring a Person's Capacity for Interaction in a Problem Solving Group," *Organizational Behavior and Human Performance* 12, no. 2 (1974): 149–69; Oliver E. Williamson, "Hierarchical Control and Optimum Firm Size," *Journal of Political Economy* 75, no. 2 (1967): 123–38.

3. Talent Acquisition: Building a Team to Propel Growth

1. Josh Bersin, "Social Recruiting Goes Wild," *Forbes*, June 22, 2012, https://www
.forbes.com/sites/joshbersin/2012/06/22/social-recruiting-goes-wild/#510132ff4764;
James Breaugh, "Talent Acquisition: A Guide to Understanding and Managing the
Recruitment Process," *SHRM Foundation*, 2016, https://www.shrm.org/hr-today/trends
-and-forecasting/special-reports-and-expert-views/documents/talent-acquisition
-recruitment.pdf.

2. Rainer Strack, Jean-Michel Caye, Carsten von der Linden, Horacio Quirós,
and Pieter Haen, "Realizing the Value of People Management," *BCG.Perspectives*,
August 2, 2012, https://www.bcg.com/en-us/publications/2012/people-management
-human-resources-leadership-from-capability-to-profitability.aspx.

3. Charles R. Greer, Jon C. Carr, and Lisa Hipp, "Strategic Staffing and Small-Firm
Performance," *Human Resource Management* 55, no. 4 (2016): 741–64.

4. Julia Levashina and Michael A. Campion, "A Model of Faking Likelihood in
the Employment Interview," *International Journal of Selection and Assessment* 14, no. 4
(2006): 299–316; Cynthia Kay Stevens and Amy L. Kristof, "Making the Right Impression:
A Field Study of Applicant Impression Management During Job Interviews," *Journal
of Applied Psychology* 80, no. 5 (1995): 587–606; Brian W. Swider, Murray R. Barrick,
T. Brad Harris, and Adam C. Stoverink, "Managing and Creating an Image in the
Interview: The Role of Interviewee Initial Impressions," *Journal of Applied Psychology*
96, no. 6 (2011): 1275–88.

5. For reviews highlighting the importance of workforce planning, we recommend
Peter Cappelli, "A Supply Chain Approach to Workforce Planning," *Organizational
Dynamics* 38, no. 1 (2009): 8–15; Mary B. Young, "Strategic Workforce Planning:
Forecasting Human Capital Needs to Execute Business Strategy," *Conference
Board*, August 2006, https://www.conference-board.org/publications/publicationdetail
.cfm?publicationid=1203.

6. Laurel A. Haycock, Patricia McCarthy, and Carol L. Skay, "Procrastination in
College Students: The Role of Self-Efficacy and Anxiety," *Journal of Counseling and
Development* 76, no. 3 (1998): 317–24.

7. Talya N. Bauer, "Onboarding New Employees: Maximizing Success," *SHRM
Foundation*, 2010, https://www.shrm.org/foundation/ourwork/initiatives/resources-from
-past-initiatives/Documents/Onboarding%20New%20Employees.pdf; Talya N. Bauer,
Todd Bodner, Berrin Erdogan, Donald M. Truxillo, and Jennifer S. Tucker, "New-
comer Adjustment During Organizational Socialization: A Meta-analytic Review of
Antecedents, Outcomes, and Methods," *Journal of Applied Psychology* 92, no. 3 (2007):
707–21; John Kammeyer-Mueller, Connie Wanberg, Alex Rubenstein, and Zhaoli Song,
"Support, Undermining, and Newcomer Socialization: Fitting in During the First
90 Days," *Academy of Management Journal* 56, no. 4 (2013): 1104–24; Alan M. Saks, Krista
L. Uggerslev, and Neil E. Fassina, "Socialization Tactics and Newcomer Adjustment:
A Meta-analytic Review and Test of a Model," *Journal of Vocational Behavior* 70, no. 3
(2007): 413–46.

8. James Breaugh, "The Contribution of Job Analysis to Recruitment," in *The Wiley Blackwell Handbook of the Psychology of Recruitment, Selection and Employee Retention* (Hoboken, NJ: Wiley, 2017), 12–28; Raymond A. Noe, John R. Hollenbeck, Barry A. Gerhart, and Patrick M. Wright, *Fundamentals of Human Resource Management*, 8th ed. (Boston: McGraw-Hill Education, 2019).

9. For additional insight into this issue, see Mark Byford, Michael D. Watkins, and Lena Triantogiannis, "Onboarding Isn't Enough," *Harvard Business Review* 95, no. 3 (2017): 78–86.

10. We want to stress that efficiency is not an excuse for laziness. An increasingly important set of concerns in startups center around diversity and inclusion shortfalls. Although early-stage startups typically will not have a formal chief diversity, equity, and inclusion (DEI) officer or be able to reasonably implement some of the high-profile DEI initiatives of their larger counterparts, this does not mean startups cannot or should not leverage a diverse talent pool as they scale. Of course, simply hiring people that do not look like or think like your majority is only a first step toward a meaningful DEI climate. For some insightful perspectives from leading scholars, we recommend Derek R. Avery and Erica N. Ruggs, "Confronting the Uncomfortable Reality of Workplace Discrimination," *MIT Sloan Management Review*, July 14, 2020, https://sloanreview .mit.edu/article/confronting-the-uncomfortable-reality-of-workplace-discrimination/; Patrick M. McKay, "Dissecting Diversity," *Catalyst* (podcast), June 22, 2020, https:// www.fox.temple.edu/catalyst/dissecting-diversity/; Quinetta Roberson, "The Science of Inclusion" (video), November 22, 2013, TEDxVillanovaU, Philadelphia, PA, https:// www.youtube.com/watch?v=SS7ID8VClko.

11. Peter Cappelli, "Your Approach to Hiring Is All Wrong," *Harvard Business Review* 97, no. 3 (2019): 48–58; Andrew Chamberlain, "Why Is Hiring Taking Longer? New Insights from Glassdoor Data," *Glassdoor*, June 18, 2015, https://www.glassdoor .com/research/time-to-hire-study/.

12. "Why and How People Change Jobs," *LinkedIn Talent Solutions*, 2015, https:// business.linkedin.com/content/dam/business/talent-solutions/global/en_us/job -switchers/PDF/job-switchers-global-report-english.pdf; Juanita Trusty, David G. Allen, and Frances Fabian, "Hunting While Working: An Expanded Model of Employed Job Search," *Human Resource Management Review* 29, no. 1 (2019): 28–42.

13. John P. Hausknecht, David V. Day, and Scott C. Thomas, "Applicant Reactions to Selection Procedures: An Updated Model and Meta-analysis," *Personnel Psychology* 57, no. 3 (2004): 639–83.

14. Talya N. Bauer, Donald M. Truxillo, Rudolph J. Sanchez, Jane M. Craig, Philip Ferrara, and Michael A. Campion, "Applicant Reactions to Selection: Development of the Selection Procedural Justice Scale (SPJS)," *Personnel Psychology* 54, no. 2 (2001): 387–419; Donald M. Truxillo, Todd E. Bodner, Marilena Bertolino, Talya N. Bauer, and Clayton A. Yonce, "Effects of Explanations on Applicant Reactions: A Meta-analytic Review," *International Journal of Selection and Assessment* 17, no. 4 (2009): 346–61; Donald M. Truxillo, Talya N. Bauer, and Alexa M. Garcia, "Applicant Reactions to Hiring Procedures," in *The Wiley Blackwell Handbook of the Psychology of Recruitment,*

Selection and Employee Retention, ed. Elaine D. Pulakos, Jonathan Passmore, and Carla Semedo (Hoboken, NJ: Wiley, 2017), 53–70.

15. Cappelli, "Your Approach to Hiring Is All Wrong," 56.

16. Adam Grant, "Goodbye to MBTI, the Fad That Won't Die," *Psychology Today*, September 18, 2013, https://www.psychologytoday.com/us/blog/give-and-take/201309 /goodbye-mbti-the-fad-won-t-die.

17. See International Personality Item Pool (website), updated September 23, 2019, https://ipip.ori.org/.

18. The trait of "conscientiousness" has proven to be a particularly stable predictor of job performance across job types (although the effect is modest). For classic summaries of research findings, we recommend Murray R. Barrick and Michael K. Mount, "The Big Five Personality Dimensions and Job Performance: A Meta-analysis," *Personnel Psychology* 44, no. 1 (1991): 1–26; Murray R. Barrick, Michael, K. Mount, and Timothy A. Judge, "The FFM Personality Dimensions and Job Performance: Meta-analysis of Meta-analyses," *International Journal of Selection and Assessment* 9, no 1–2 (2001): 9–30.

19. For a review of the scientific literature on referrals, including the upsides and downsides of such practices, see Steven D. Schlachter and Jenna R. Pieper, "Employee Referral Hiring in Organizations: An Integrative Conceptual Review, Model, and Agenda for Future Research," *Journal of Applied Psychology* 104, no. 11 (2019): 1325–46.

20. Derek R. Avery, Patrick F. McKay, and Sabrina D. Volpone, "Diversity Staffing: Inclusive Personnel Recruitment and Selection Practices," in The Oxford Handbook of Diversity and Work, ed. Quinetta M. Roberson (Oxford: Oxford University Press, 2013), 282–99; Quinetta M. Roberson, "Diversity in the Workplace: A Review, Synthesis, and Future Research Agenda," *Annual Review of Organizational Psychology and Organizational Behavior* 6 (2019): 69–88.

4. Total Rewards: Creating a Compelling Employment Value Proposition

1. Gartner, "Strengthen Your Employee Value Proposition," accessed July 23, 2020, https://www.gartner.com/en/human-resources/insights/employee-engagement -performance/employee-value-proposition.

2. Kerry Jones, "Employee Benefits Study: The Cost and Value of Employee Perks," *Fractl* (blog), June 10, 2020, http://www.frac.tl/employee-benefits-study/; Kerry Jones, "The Most Desirable Employee Benefits," *Harvard Business Review*, February 15, 2017, https://hbr.org/2017/02/the-most-desirable-employee-benefits.

3. Mercer, "The Modern Employee Value Proposition: Compensation Is the Foundation," September 24, 2019.

4. Peter Cappelli, "A Market-Driven Approach to Retaining Talent," *Harvard Business Review* 78, no. 1 (2000): 103–11.

5. For scholarly insight into general pay dispersion effects, see Matt Bloom, "The Performance Effects of Pay Dispersion on Individuals and Organizations," *Academy of Management Journal* 42, no. 1 (1999): 25–40; James W. Fredrickson, Alison Davis-Blake, and W. M. Gerard Sanders, "Sharing the Wealth: Social Comparisons and Pay Dispersion in the CEO's Top Team," *Strategic Management Journal* 31, no. 10 (2010): 1031–53; Jason D. Shaw, "Pay Dispersion," *Annual Review of Organizational Psychology and Organizational Behavior* 1, no. 1 (2014): 521–44. We note also that differentiated initial pay offerings can have significant effects on DEI issues later. The following sources provide helpful information on these issues: Derek R. Avery and Patrick F. McKay, "Doing Diversity Right: An Empirically Based Approach to Effective Diversity Management," in the *International Review of Industrial and Organization Psychology*, ed. Gerard P. Hodgkinson and Kevin Ford (Indianapolis: Wiley, 2010): 25:227–52; PayScale, "Does Pay Transparency Close the Gender Wage Gap," accessed July 23, 2020, https://www.payscale.com/data/pay-transparency.

6. Mark C. Bolino, K. Michele Kacmar, William H. Turnley, and J. Bruce Gilstrap, "A Multi-Level Review of Impression Management Motives and Behaviors," *Journal of Management* 34, no. 5 (2008): 1080–1109; Cynthia Kay Stevens and Amy L. Kristof, "Making the Right Impression: A Field Study of Applicant Impression Management During Job Interviews," *Journal of Applied Psychology* 80, no. 5 (1995): 587–606; Brent Weiss and Robert S. Feldman, "Looking Good and Lying to Do It: Deception as an Impression Management Strategy in Job Interviews," *Journal of Applied Social Psychology* 36, no. 4 (2006): 1070–86.

7. Robert E. Carlson, "Selection Interview Decisions: The Effect of Interviewer Experience, Relative Quota Situation, and Applicant Sample on Interviewer Decisions," *Personnel Psychology* 20, no. 4 (1967): 259–80; Rachel E. Frieder, Chad H. Van Iddekinge, and Patrick H. Raymark, "How Quickly Do Interviewers Reach Decisions? An Examination of Interviewers' Decision-Making Time Across Applicants," *Journal of Occupational and Organizational Psychology* 89, no. 2 (2016): 223–48; Laura Huang, Marcia Frideger, and Jone L. Pearce, "Political Skill: Explaining the Effects of Nonnative Accent on Managerial Hiring and Entrepreneurial Investment Decisions," *Journal of Applied Psychology* 98, no. 6 (2013): 1005–17; Cynthia M. Marlowe, Sandra L. Schneider, and Carnot E. Nelson, "Gender and Attractiveness Biases in Hiring Decisions: Are More Experienced Managers Less Biased?," *Journal of Applied Psychology* 81, no. 1 (1996): 11–21; Sharon L. Segrest Purkiss, Pamela L. Perrewé, Treena L. Gillespie, Bronston T. Mayes, and Gerald R. Ferris, "Implicit Sources of Bias in Employment Interview Judgments and Decisions," *Organizational Behavior and Human Decision Processes* 101, no. 2 (2006): 152–67; Lauren A. Rivera, "Hiring as Cultural Matching: The Case of Elite Professional Service Firms," *American Sociological Review* 77, no. 6 (2012): 999–1022.

8. Gartner Says Companies in the U.S. Are Overpaying To Attract New Talent," June 11, 2019, https://www.gartner.com/en/newsroom/press-releases/2019-06-11-gartner-says-companies-in-the-u-s--are-overpaying-to-

9. See Barry Gerhart and Jerry M. Newman, *Compensation*, 13th ed. (New York: McGraw-Hill, 2020).

10. Jones, "Employee Benefits Study"; SHRM.org, "Healthcare and Health Services: SHRM Employee Benefits 2019," June 2019, https://www.shrm.org/hr-today/trends-and -forecasting/research-and-surveys/Documents/SHRM%20Employee%20Benefits%20 2019%20Healthcare%20and%20Health%20Services.pdf.

11. One of our favorite brokers is Sequoia, based in San Francisco, which has a unique depth of experience in supporting high-growth organizations and operates a popular professional employer organization (PEO). Melita Group, out of San Jose, is also a solid option for a benefits broker, offering a variety of additional HR administration outsourcing packages.

12. Kaiser Family Foundation, "2019 Employer Health Benefits Survey," September 25, 2019, https://www.kff.org/report-section/ehbs-2019-section-1-cost-of-health -insurance/.

13. NetPEO, "How Much Does It Cost to Use a PEO?," accessed July 27, 2020, https://www.netpeo.com/faqs/how-much-does-it-cost-to-use-a-peo/.

14. " 'Don't Touch My Perks': Companies That Eliminate Them Risk Employee Backlash," *K@W* (blog), July 23, 2008, https://knowledge.wharton.upenn.edu/article /dont-touch-my-perks-companies-that-eliminate-them-risk-employee-backlash/.

15. Daniel Kahneman, Jack L. Knetsch, and Richard H. Thaler, "Anomalies: The Endowment Effect, Loss Aversion, and Status Quo Bias," *Journal of Economic Perspectives* 5, no. 1 (1991): 193–206.

16. " 'Don't Touch My Perks.'"

17. For more on the pros and cons of benefits such as free lunches, see Jones, "Employee Benefits Study." We also want to acknowledge that work from home issues may be changing in large part due to the COVID-19 pandemic, although the staying power of these changes is as yet unknown. For a representative glimpse of the extant scholarly literature on this topic, see Ravi S. Gajendran and David A. Harrison, "The Good, the Bad, and the Unknown About Telecommuting: Meta-analysis of Psychological Mediators and Individual Consequences," *Journal of Applied Psychology* 92, no. 6 (2007): 1524–41; Gretchen M. Spreitzer, Lindsey Cameron, and Lyndon Garrett, "Alternative Work Arrangements: Two Images of the New World of Work," *Annual Review of Organizational Psychology and Organizational Behavior* 4 (2017): 473–99.

18. AngelList (website), https://angel.co/salaries.

19. Wealthfront (blog), https://blog.wealthfront.com/startup-employee-equity -compensation/.

20. Advanced HR (website), https://www.advanced-hr.com/.

21. Radford, "Private Company Survey," https://radford.aon.com/surveys.

22. For an excellent example, see Sue Shellenbarger, "The Dangers of Hiring for Cultural Fit," *Wall Street Journal*, September 23, 2019, https://www.wsj.com/articles /the-dangers-of-hiring-for-cultural-fit-11569231000.

23. See Gartner, "Strengthen Your Employee Value Proposition."

24. Mercer, "2020 Global Talent Trends," https://www.mercer.com/our-thinking /career/global-talent-hr-trends.html#contactForm; Mercer, "Preparing for the Future of Work: Evaluating the Effectiveness of Your Employee Value Proposition," September 14,

2018, https://www.mercer.com/our-thinking/career/voice-on-talent/preparing-for-the -future-of-work-evaluating-the-effectiveness-your-employee-value-proposition.html.

25. Sydney Finkelstein, "Why a One-Size-Fits-All Approach to Employee Development Doesn't Work," *Harvard Business Review*, March 5, 2019, https://hbr.org /2019/03/why-a-one-size-fits-all-approach-to-employee-development-doesnt-work.

5. Learning and Development: Core and Strategic Investments

1. Josh Bersin, *Rethinking the Build vs Buy Approach to Talent: How Savvy Employers Are Building Tech Skills from Within*, Whiteboard Advisors, 2019, 21, https://joshbersin .com/wp-content/uploads/2019/10/Build_vs_buy_Bersin_1.0.pdf.

2. "Building Organizational Capabilities: McKinsey Global Survey Results," *McKinsey & Company*, March 1, 2010, https://www.mckinsey.com/business-functions /organization/our-insights/building-organizational-capabilities-mckinsey-global -survey-results.

3. Steve Glaveski, "Where Companies Go Wrong with Learning and Development," *Harvard Business Review*, October 2, 2019, https://hbr.org/2019/10/where -companies-go-wrong-with-learning-and-development.

4. Laszlo Bock, "You Learn Best When You Learn Less," *Harvard Business Review*, June 17, 2019, https://hbr.org/2019/06/you-learn-best-when-you-learn-less.

5. Bradford S. Bell, Scott I. Tannenbaum, J. Kevin Ford, Raymond A. Noe, and Kurt Kraiger, "100 Years of Training and Development Research: What We Know and Where We Should Go," *Journal of Applied Psychology* 102, no. 3 (2017): 305–23; Irwin L. Goldstein and J. Kevin Ford, *Training in Organizations: Needs Assessment, Development, and Evaluation*, 4th ed. (Belmont, CA: Wadsworth, 2002).

6. Raymond Noe, "Learning System Design: A Guide to Effective Learning Initia- tives," *SHRM Foundation*, 2009, https://www.shrm.org/hr-today/trends-and-forecasting /special-reports-and-expert-views/Documents/Learning-System-Design.pdf.

7. Brian W. Swider, Murray R. Barrick, and T. Brad Harris, "Initial Impressions: What They Are, What They Are Not, and How They Influence Structured Interview Outcomes," *Journal of Applied Psychology* 101, no. 5 (2016): 625–38.

8. A helpful guide for those new to structured interviews is "A Guide to Con- ducting Behavioral Interviews with Early Job Candidates," SHRM *Foundation*, 2016, https://www.shrm.org/LearningAndCareer/learning/Documents/Behavioral%20 Interviewing%20Guide%20for%20Early%20Career%20Candidates.pdf. For additional reading on how to improve the validity of interviews, see Iris Bohnet, "How to Take the Bias Out of Interviews," *Harvard Business Review*, April 18, 2016, https://hbr.org /2016/04/how-to-take-the-bias-out-of-interviews; Michael A. Campion, Elliott D. Pursell, and Barbara K. Brown, "Structured Interviewing: Raising the Psychometric Properties of the Employment Interview," *Personnel Psychology* 41, no. 1 (1988): 25–42.

9. Scott Highhouse, "Stubborn Reliance on Intuition and Subjectivity in Employee Selection," *Industrial and Organizational Psychology* 1, no. 3 (2008): 333–42; Allen I.

Huffcutt and Winfred Arthur, "Hunter and Hunter (1984) Revisited: Interview Validity for Entry-Level Jobs," *Journal of Applied Psychology* 79, no. 2 (1994): 184–90; Julia Levashina, Christopher J. Hartwell, Frederick P. Morgeson, and Michael A. Campion, "The Structured Employment Interview: Narrative and Quantitative Review of the Research Literature," *Personnel Psychology* 67, no. 1 (2014): 241–93.

10. Talya N. Bauer and Stephen G. Green, "Testing the Combined Effects of Newcomer Information Seeking and Manager Behavior on Socialization," *Journal of Applied Psychology* 83, no. 1 (1998): 72–83; Ning Li, T. Brad Harris, Wendy R. Boswell, and Zhitao Xie, "The Role of Organizational Insiders' Developmental Feedback and Proactive Personality on Newcomers' Performance: An Interactionist Perspective," *Journal of Applied Psychology* 96, no. 6 (2011): 1317–27.

11. Talya N. Bauer, "Onboarding New Employees: Maximizing Success," *SHRM Foundation*, 2010, https://www.shrm.org/foundation/ourwork/initiatives/resources-from -past-initiatives/Documents/Onboarding%20New%20Employees.pdf; Gallup, "Create an Exceptional Onboarding Journey for Your New Employees," 2019, https://www .gallup.com/workplace/247076/onboarding-new-employees-perspective-paper.aspx.

12. Roy Maurer, "Onboarding Key to Retaining, Engaging Talent," *SHRM Foundation*, April 16, 2015, https://www.shrm.org/resourcesandtools/hr-topics/talent -acquisition/pages/onboarding-key-retaining-engaging-talent.aspx.

13. For scholarly reviews of newcomer onboarding/socialization research, see Tammy D. Allen, Lillian T. Eby, Georgia T. Chao, and Talya N. Bauer, "Taking Stock of Two Relational Aspects of Organizational Life: Tracing the History and Shaping the Future of Socialization and Mentoring Research," *Journal of Applied Psychology* 102, no. 3 (2017): 324–37; Talya N. Bauer, Todd Bodner, Berrin Erdogan, Donald M. Truxillo, and Jennifer S. Tucker, "Newcomer Adjustment During Organizational Socialization: A Meta-analytic Review of Antecedents, Outcomes, and Methods," *Journal of Applied Psychology* 92, no. 3 (2007): 707–21; Ruolian Fang, Michelle K. Duffy, and Jason D. Shaw, "The Organizational Socialization Process: Review and Development of a Social Capital Model," *Journal of Management* 37, no. 1 (2011): 127–52; Alan M. Saks, Krista L. Uggerslev, and Neil E. Fassina, "Socialization Tactics and Newcomer Adjustment: A Meta-analytic Review and Test of a Model," *Journal of Vocational Behavior* 70, no. 3 (2007): 413–46.

14. Bauer, "Onboarding New Employees."

15. Newcomer onboarding and socialization efforts may be particularly beneficial in advancing DEI efforts. For an insightful perspective on this issue, see Charlice Hurst, John Kammeyer-Mueller, and Beth Livingston, "The Odd One Out: How Newcomers Who Are Different Become Adjusted," in *The Oxford Handbook of Organizational Socialization*, ed. Connie Wanberg (New York: Oxford University Press, 2012), 115–38.

16. Bradley L. Kirkman and T. Brad Harris, *3D Team Leadership: A New Approach for Complex Teams* (Stanford, CA: Stanford University Press, 2017).

17. Yoram Solomon, "Why Google's '20 Percent' Rule Is Actually Useless," *Inc.com*, March 10, 2016, https://www.inc.com/yoram-solomon/20-of-my-time-will-not-make -me-more-creative.html.

18. For an interesting take on this issue, see Ron Carucci, "When Companies Should Invest in Training Their Employees—And When They Shouldn't," *Harvard Business Review*, October 29, 2018, https://hbr.org/2018/10/when-companies-should-invest-in-training-their-employees-and-when-they-shouldnt.

19. Related frameworks use the terms "Ability Motivation Opportunity" and "Have Feel Do." For a deeper dive, see Eileen Appelbaum, Thomas Bailey, Peter Berg, Arne L. Kalleberg, and Thomas Andrew Bailey, *Manufacturing Advantage: Why High-Performance Work Systems Pay Off* (Ithaca, NY: Cornell University Press, 2000); David P. Lepak, Hui Liao, Yunhyung Chung, and Erika E. Harden, "A Conceptual Review of Human Resource Management Systems in Strategic Human Resource Management Research," *Research in Personnel and Human Resources Management* 25, no. 1 (2006): 217–71; Patrick Wright, "Human Resource Strategy: Adapting to the Age of Globalization," *SHRM Foundation*, 2008, https://www.shrm.org/hr-today/trends-and-forecasting/special-reports-and-expert-views/Documents/HR-Strategy-Globalization.pdf.

20. Noe, "Learning System Design."

21. Charles R. Greer, Stuart A. Youngblood, and David A. Gray, "Human Resource Management Outsourcing: The Make or Buy Decision," *Academy of Management Perspectives* 13, no. 3 (1999): 85–96.

22. Arthur Winfred Jr., Winston Bennett Jr., Pamela S. Edens, and Suzanne T. Bell, "Effectiveness of Training in Organizations: A Meta-analysis of Design and Evaluation Features," *Journal of Applied Psychology* 88, no. 2 (2003): 234–45; Bell et al., "100 Years of Training and Development Research"; Brian D. Blume, J. Kevin Ford, Timothy T. Baldwin, and Jason L. Huang, "Transfer of Training: A Meta-analytic Review," *Journal of Management* 36, no. 4 (2010): 1065–1105.

6. Culture, Engagement, and Communications: Creating the Environment for Success

1. Edgar Schein, "Organizational Culture," *American Psychologist* 45, no. 2 (1990): 109–19.

2. Boris Groysberg, Jeremiah Lee, Jesse Price, and J. Cheng, "The Leader's Guide to Corporate Culture," *Harvard Business Review* 96, no. 1 (January–February 2018): 45.

3. Schein, "Organizational Culture," 111.

4. Benjamin Schneider, "The People Make the Place," *Personnel Psychology* 40, no. 3 (1987): 437–53.

5. Larry E. Greiner, "Evolution and Revolution as Organizations Grow," *Harvard Business Review* 76, no. 3 (May–June 1998): 55–64; Schneider, "The People Make the Place."

6. Robin I. M. Dunbar, "Coevolution of Neocortical Size, Group Size, and Language in Humans," *Behavioral and Brain Sciences* 16, no. 4 (1993): 681–94; Russell A. Hill and Robin I. M. Dunbar, "Social Network Size in Humans," *Human Nature* 14, no. 1 (2003): 53–72.

7. Sam G. B. Roberts, Robin I. M. Dunbar, Thomas V. Pollet, and Toon Kuppens, "Exploring Variation in Active Network Size: Constraints and Ego Characteristics," *Social Networks* 31, no. 2 (2009): 138–46.

8. Barry M. Staw, Lance E. Sandelands, and Jane E. Dutton, "Threat Rigidity Effects in Organizational Behavior: A Multilevel Analysis," *Administrative Science Quarterly* 26, no. 4 (1981): 501–24.

9. Elizabeth Briody, Tracy Meerwarth Pester, and Robert Trotter, "A Story's Impact on Organizational-Culture Change," *Journal of Organizational Change Management* 25, no. 1 (2012): 67–87.

10. Although some of former celebrity CEO Jack Welch's management practices have not aged well and would be inappropriate in a startup context, we find that his (along with coauthor Suzy Welch's) practical advice on mission and values is still timely. Jack Welch and Suzy Welch, *Winning* (New York: HarperCollins, 2005), 13–24.

11. Jim Collins, *Good to Great: Why Some Companies Make the Leap . . . and Others Don't* (New York: HarperBusiness, 2001).

12. For an insightful, inspiring, and highly practical discussion related to this topic, we recommend Professor Laura Huang's (Harvard) recent book: Laura Huang, *Edge: Turning Adversity Into Advantage* (New York: Portfolio/Penguin, 2020).

13. Julia E. Hoch, William H. Bommer, James H. Dulebohn, and Dongyuan Wu, "Do Ethical, Authentic, and Servant Leadership Explain Variance Above and Beyond Transformational Leadership? A Meta-analysis," *Journal of Management* 44, no. 2 (2018): 501–29.

14. Many organizations, including startups, are rightfully placing more value on having a diverse and inclusive climate. Consistent with our belief that actions speak louder than words, well-known HR scholar Patrick McKay (Temple University) recently spoke about how leaders often "fetishize" DEI initiatives, noting specifically that "they think it's this magical thing that's going to result in all of these great outcomes. Not realizing the work it takes to truly implement it well. I think people underestimate it. They really think it's this easy thing, they can say the right things, they can say the right words—and not realize that involves embodying the principles behind it and the work that it takes and the commitment it takes to changing a company philosophy in terms of how to do business." Patrick M. McKay, "Dissecting Diversity," *Catalyst* (podcast), June 22, 2020, https://www.fox.temple.edu/catalyst/dissecting-diversity/. For comprehensive scholarly references, see Quinetta M. Roberson, Ed., *The Oxford Handbook of Diversity and Work* (New York: Oxford University Press, 2013); Quinetta Roberson, Ann Marie Ryan, and Belle Rose Ragins, "The Evolution and Future of Diversity at Work," *Journal of Applied Psychology* 102, no. 3 (2017): 483–99.

15. Biz Carson, "Exclusive Investigation: How Lies and a Troubled Workplace Brought Down the Founder of $115 Million Cleo," *Forbes*, Jun 18, 2019, https://www.forbes.com/sites/bizcarson/2019/06/18/exclusive-investigation-how-lies-and-a-troubled-workplace-brought-down-shannon-spanhake-cleo/#2d1cfa2c7608.

16. Soroush Vosoughi, Deb Roy, and Sinan Aral, "The Spread of True and False News Online," *Science* 359, no. 6380 (2018): 1146–51.

17. This lesson has been developed and confirmed largely in a marketing context, although we believe it generalizes to general management communication as well. For a quantitative review of "effective frequency" research, see Susanne Schmidt and Martin Eisend, "Advertising Repetition: A Meta-analysis on Effective Frequency in Advertising," *Journal of Advertising* 44, no. 4 (2015): 415–28.

18. Ashish Mahajan, James W. Bishop, and Dow Scott, "Does Trust in Top Management Mediate Top Management Communication, Employee Involvement, and Organizational Commitment Relationships?," *Journal of Managerial Issues* 24, no. 2 (2012): 173–90.

19. For a review of the positive benefits of creating a psychologically safe environment, see Amy C. Edmondson and Zhike Lei, "Psychological Safety: The History, Renaissance, and Future of an Interpersonal Construct," *Annual Review of Organizational Psychology and Organizational Behavior* 1, no. 1 (2014): 23–43.

20. Peter Cappelli and Liat Eldor, "Where Measuring Engagement Goes Wrong," *Harvard Business Review*, May 17, 2019, https://hbr.org/2019/05/where-measuring -engagement-goes-wrong.

21. Gallup, "Gallup Q12 Employee Engagement Survey," accessed July 23, 2020, https://q12.gallup.com/Public/en-us/Features.

22. OfficeVibe, "12 Mind-Blowing Employee Survey Statistics," September 9, 2014, https://officevibe.com/blog/employee-surveys-infographic.

7. Performance Management and Goal Setting: Clarity, Consistency, and Consequences

1. Ben Wigert and Jim Harter, "Re-Engineering Performance Management," *Gallup*, 2017, https://www.gallup.com/workplace/238064/re-engineering-performance -management.aspx.

2. Angelo S. DeNisi and Kevin R. Murphy, "Performance Appraisal and Performance Management: 100 Years of Progress?," *Journal of Applied Psychology* 102, no. 3 (2017): 421.

3. Karen Martin, *The Outstanding Organization: Generate Business Results by Eliminating Chaos and Building the Foundation for Everyday Excellence* (New York: McGraw-Hill, 2012), 18–19.

4. Ning Li, Xiaoming Zheng, T. Brad Harris, Xin Liu, and Bradley L. Kirkman, "Recognizing 'Me' Benefits 'We': Investigating the Positive Spillover Effects of Formal Individual Recognition in Teams," *Journal of Applied Psychology* 101, no. 7 (2016): 925–39; Alexander D. Stajkovic and Fred Luthans, "Differential Effects of Incentive Motivators on Work Performance," *Academy of Management Journal* 44, no. 3 (2001): 580–90.

5. Ad Kleingeld, Heleen van Mierlo, and Lidia Arends, "The Effect of Goal Setting on Group Performance: A Meta-analysis," *Journal of Applied Psychology* 96, no. 6 (2011): 1289–1304; Edwin A. Locke and Gary P. Latham, *A Theory of Goal Setting and Task*

Performance (Upper Saddle River, NJ: Prentice-Hall, 1990); Edwin A. Locke and Gary P. Latham, "New Directions in Goal-Setting Theory," *Current Directions in Psychological Science* 15, no. 5 (2006): 265–68.

6. Geoge T. Doran, "There's a SMART Way to Write Management's Goals and Objectives," *Management Review* 70, no. 11 (1981): 35–36.

7. For instance, FAST goals (Frequently discussed, Ambitious, Specific, Transparent). See Donald Sull and Charles Sull, "With Goals, FAST beats SMART," *MIT Sloan Management Review* 59, no. 4 (2018): 1–11.

8. Patrick Lencioni, *The Advantage: Why Organizational Health Trumps Everything Else in Business* (San Francisco, CA: Jossey-Bass, 2012).

9. For an origin story on OKRs, see Andrew S. Grove, *High Output Management* (New York: Vintage, 2015).

10. Avraham N. Kluger and Angelo DeNisi, "The Effects of Feedback Interventions on Performance: A Historical Review, a Meta-analysis, and a Preliminary Feedback Intervention Theory," *Psychological Bulletin* 119, no. 2 (1996): 254–84.

11. For examples of why companies have opted to remove performance ratings, see Leonardo Baldassarre and Brian Finken, "GE's Real-Time Performance Development," *Harvard Business Review*, August 12, 2015, https://hbr.org/2015/08/ges-real-time-performance-development; Samuel Culbert, "Get Rid of the Performance Review!," *Wall Street Journal*, October 20, 2008, https://www.wsj.com/articles/SB122426318874844933; David Rock, Josh Davis, and Beth Jones, "Kill Your Performance Ratings," *Strategy+ Business* 76 (Autumn 2014), https://www.strategy-business.com/article/00275?gko=586a5.

12. For more discussion on this issue, see Peter Cappelli and Anna Tavis, "The Performance Management Revolution," *Harvard Business Review* 94, no. 10 (October 2016): 58–67; Lori Goler, Janelle Gale, and Adam Grant, "Let's Not Kill Performance Evaluations Yet," *Harvard Business Review* 94, no. 11 (November 2016): 90–94.

13. Michael P. O'Driscoll and Terry A. Beehr, "Supervisor Behaviors, Role Stressors and Uncertainty as Predictors of Personal Outcomes for Subordinates," *Journal of Organizational Behavior* 15, no. 2 (1994): 141–55.

14. DeNisi and Murphy, "Performance Appraisal and Performance Management: 100 Years of Progress?"

15. Robert Sutton and Ben Wigert, "More Harm Than Good: The Truth About Performance Reviews," *Gallup*, May 6, 2019, https://www.gallup.com/workplace/249332/harm-good-truth-performance-reviews.aspx.

16. Rebecca Knight, "How to Make Your One-on-Ones with Employees More Productive," *Harvard Business Review*, August 8, 2016, https://hbr.org/2016/08/how-to-make-your-one-on-ones-with-employees-more-productive.

17. Grove, *High Output Management*, 74.

18. Our point here is not to denigrate neuroscience applications at work (indeed, many very smart people are working on this topic) but to highlight that the jury is still very much out on the value of some popular prescriptions. For academic reviews, see Neal M. Ashkanasy, William J. Becker, and David A. Waldman, "Neuroscience and Organizational Behavior: Avoiding Both Neuro-euphoria and Neuro-phobia," *Journal of*

Organizational Behavior 35, no. 7 (2014): 909–19; Anthony I. Jack, Kylie C. Rochford, Jared P. Friedman, Angela M. Passarelli, and Richard E. Boyatzis, "Pitfalls in Organizational Neuroscience: A Critical Review and Suggestions for Future Research," *Organizational Research Methods* 22, no. 1 (2019): 421–58; Nick Lee, Carl Senior, and Michael J. R. Butler, "The Domain of Organizational Cognitive Neuroscience: Theoretical and Empirical Challenges," *Journal of Management* 38, no. 4 (2012): 921–31; Dirk Lindebaum, "Critical Essay: Building New Management Theories on Sound Data? The Case of Neuroscience," *Human Relations* 69, no. 3 (2016): 537–50.

On a lighter note, some research has even identified brain activity in dead fish using common research techniques. Craig M. Bennet, Abigail A. Baird, Michael B. Miller, and George L. Wolford, "Neural Correlates of Interspecies Perspective Taking in the Post-mortem Atlantic Salmon: An Argument for Proper Multiple Comparisons Correction" (poster), 15th Annual Meeting for Human Brain Mapping, San Francisco, CA, June 2009, http://prefrontal.org/files/posters/Bennett-Salmon-2009.pdf.

19. For classic reviews, see Edward E. Lawler, *Pay and Organization Effectiveness: A Psychological View* (New York: McGraw Hill, 1971); Sara L. Rynes, Barry Gerhart, and Laura Parks, "Personnel Psychology: Performance Evaluation and Pay for Performance," *Annual Review of Psychology* 56 (2005): 571–600.

20. PayScale, "The 2020 Compensation Best Practices: Winning the Juggling Act: How Strategic Compensation Attracts and Retains Top Talent in a Tightening Labor Market," 2020, https://www.payscale.com/cbpr#topperformers.

21. Li et al., "Recognizing 'Me' Benefits 'We.'"

22. For a research-backed treatment of transparency, see Peter Bamberger and Elena Belogolovsky, "The Impact of Pay Secrecy on Individual Task Performance," *Personnel Psychology* 63, no. 4 (2010): 965–96; Peter Bamberger and Elena Belogolovsky, "The Dark Side of Transparency: How and When Pay Administration Practices Affect Employee Helping," *Journal of Applied Psychology* 102, no. 4 (2017): 658–71.

8. Legal and Compliance: Common Traps and Easy Answers

1. Chenwei Liao, Sandy J. Wayne, and Denise M. Rousseau, "Idiosyncratic Deals in Contemporary Organizations: A Qualitative and Meta-analytical Review," *Journal of Organizational Behavior* 37, no. S1 (2016), S9–S29; Denise Rousseau, *I-Deals: Idiosyncratic Deals Employees Bargain for Themselves* (New York: Sharpe, 2005); Denise M. Rousseau, Violet T. Ho, and Jerald Greenberg, "I-Deals: Idiosyncratic Terms in Employment Relationships," *Academy of Management Review* 31, no. 4 (2006): 977–94.

2. Teresa Brady, "Employee Handbooks: Contracts or Empty Promises?," *Management Review* 82, no. 6 (1993): 33–35.

3. For example, California requires two hours of sexual harassment prevention training every two years for supervisory employers; https://leginfo.legislature.ca.gov/faces/billNavClient.xhtml?bill_id=200320040AB1825.

4. For more details, see "Private Attorneys General Act (PAGA)—Filing," State of California Department of Industrial Relations, accessed July 24, 2020, https://www.dir.ca.gov/Private-Attorneys-General-Act/Private-Attorneys-General-Act.html.

5. Maria Y. Robbins, "Overtime Exemption for Computer Software Employees" (public memo), State of California Department of Industrial Relations, October 22, 2019, https://www.dir.ca.gov/OPRL/ComputerSoftware.pdf.

6. U.S. Department of Labor Wage and Hour Division (website), https://www.dol.gov/whd/.

7. California labor policies websites include "Wage Claim Adjudication," State of California Department of Industrial Relations, Division of Labor Standards Enforcement, accessed July 24, 2020, https://www.dir.ca.gov/dlse/dlseWagesAndHours.html; "Exemptions from the Overtime Laws," State of California Department of Industrial Relations, Division of Labor Standards Enforcement, accessed July 24, 2020, https://www.dir.ca.gov/dlse/FAQ_OvertimeExemptions.htm.

8. Many professional organizations offer additional guidance on differentiating between employees and contractors. Robert W. Wood, "Do's and Don'ts When Using Independent Contractors," *Business Law Today*, June 2011, https://www.americanbar.org/groups/business_law/publications/blt/2011/06/03_wood/.

9. As an example, a status inquiry in California could involve the Division of Labor Standards Enforcement, Employment Development Department, Division of Workers' Compensation, Franchise Tax Board, and the Contractors State Licensing Board.

10. "Fact Sheet 13: Employment Relationship Under the Fair Labor Standards Act (FLSA)," U.S. Department of Labor Wage and Hour Division, accessed July 27, 2020, https://www.dol.gov/agencies/whd/fact-sheets/13-flsa-employment-relationship.

11. Professional HR organizations (including SHRM) maintain a database of helpful resources and toolkits. See "Involuntary Termination of Employment in the United States," *SHRM Foundation*, August 24, 2018, https://www.shrm.org/resourcesandtools/tools-and-samples/toolkits/pages/involuntaryterminationof.aspx; "Termination Checklist," *SHRM Foundation*, accessed July 23, 2020, https://www.shrm.org/resourcesandtools/tools-and-samples/hr-forms/pages/cms_002039.aspx.

9. How and When to Construct Your People Team: Supporting Your Scale-Up

1. "Why Chief Human Resources Officers Make Great CEOs," *Harvard Business Review* 93, no. 3 (December 2014): 30–32.

2. Drew Hansen, "How VCs Deploy Operating Talent to Build Better Startups," *Forbes*, December 26, 2012, https://www.forbes.com/sites/drewhansen/2012/12/26/how-vcs-deploy-operating-talent-to-build-better-startups/#31c1fa6036ef; Dave Ulrich and Justin Allen, "PE Firms Are Creating a New Role: Leadership Capital Partner," *Harvard Business Review*, August 11, 2017, https://hbr.org/2017/08/pe-firms-are-creating-a-new-role-leadership-capital-partner; Reed Flesher, "VC Talent Partners: Adding Value to

Their Portfolio Companies," *Thrive*, January 4, 2016, https://thrivetrm.com/vc-talent -partners-adding-value-to-the-portfolio-companies/.

3. Josh Bersin, "HR Technology: The Dirty Little Secret," *JoshBersin.com*, updated November 22, 2019, https://joshbersin.com/2019/11/hr-technology-the-dirty -little-secret/.

4. For more interesting (and troubling) reading on the disconnect between common HR tendencies and evidence-based practices, see Sara L. Rynes, Amy E. Colbert, and Ernest H. O'Boyle, "When the 'Best Available Evidence' Doesn't Win: How Doubts About Science and Scientists Threaten the Future of Evidence-based Management," *Journal of Management* 44, no. 8 (2018): 2995–3010; Sara L. Rynes and Jean M. Bartunek, "Evidence-based Management: Foundations, Development, Controversies and Future," *Annual Review of Organizational Psychology and Organizational Behavior* 4 (2017): 235–61.

5. Gartner, "Gartner Magic Quadrant," accessed July 24, 2020, https://www.gartner .com/en/research/methodologies/magic-quadrants-research.

6. For other helpful resources, see software reviews and buyers' guides for business technology at G2Crowd Source, Trust Radius, and Forrester Wave.

10. Where Next?

1. Larry E. Greiner, "Evolution and Revolution as Organizations Grow," *Harvard Business Review* 76, no. 3 (May–June 1998): 55–64.

2. For an interesting discussion on this issue, see Elad Gil, "Managing the Board," chap. 2 in *High Growth Handbook* (San Francisco: Stripe, 2018).

3. Reid Hoffman and Chris Yeh, *Blitzscaling: The Lightning-Fast Path to Building Massively Valuable Businesses* (New York: Broadway Business, 2018).

4. Mark Zuckerberg, "Imperfect Is Perfect," interview by Reid Hoffman, *Masters of Scale* (podcast), May 24, 2017, https://mastersofscale.com/mark-zuckerberg-imperfect -is-perfect/.

5. Bradley L. Kirkman and T. Brad Harris, *3D Team Leadership: A New Approach for Complex Teams* (Stanford, CA: Stanford University Press, 2017).

6. Kurt T. Dirks and Donald L. Ferrin, "The Role of Trust in Organizational Settings," *Organization Science* 12, no. 4 (2001): 450–67; Gail Fann Thomas, Roxanne Zolin, and Jackie L. Hartman, "The Central Role of Communication in Developing Trust and Its Effect on Employee Involvement," *Journal of Business Communication* 46, no. 3 (June 2009): 287–310.

7. John P. Kotter, "Leading Change: Why Transformation Efforts Fail," *Harvard Business Review* 73, no. 2 (March–April 1995): 59–67.

8. Greiner, "Evolution and Revolution."

9. For more on this issue, see Aaron Harris, "Who Should Founders Listen to for Advice?" (blog video), December 6, 2019, https://blog.ycombinator.com /who-should-founders-listen-to-for-advice/.

10. People Tech Partners (website), https://peopletechpartners.com/; Startup Experts (website), https://www.startupexperts.us/.

FURTHER READING

Attiyah, Ray. *Run Improve Grow: Your Roadmap from Firefighting to Bold Business Growth*. Brookline, MA: Bibliomotion, 2013.

Blumberg, Matt. *Startup CEO: A Field Guide to Scaling Up Your Business*. Hoboken, NJ: Wiley, 2013.

Burchell, Michael, and Jennifer Robin. *The Great Workplace: How to Build It, How to Keep It, and Why It Matters*. San Francisco, CA: Jossey-Bass, 2010.

Charam, Ram, Dominic Barton, and Denis Carey. *Talent Wins: The New Playbook for Putting People First*. Brighton, MA: Harvard Business Review Press, 2018.

Draper, Tim. *How to Be the Startup Hero: A Guide and Textbook for Entrepreneurs and Aspiring Entrepreneurs*. Kindle Direct Publishing, 2017.

Effron, Marc, and Miriam Ort. *One Page Talent Management: Eliminating Complexity, Adding Value*. Boston, MA: Harvard Business Review Press, 2010.

Ellis, Sean, and Morgan Brown. *Hacking Growth: How Today's Fastest-Growing Companies Drive Breakout Success*. New York: Crown, 2017.

Gil, Elad. *High Growth Handbook: Scaling Startups from 10 to 10,000 People*. San Francisco, CA: Stripe, 2018.

Harnish, Verne. *Scaling Up: How a Few Companies Make It . . . and Why the Rest Don't*. Ashburn, VA: Gazelles, 2014.

Hill, Linda, and Kent Lineback. *Being the Boss: The 3 Imperatives for Becoming a Great Leader*. Boston, MA: Harvard Business Review Press, 2011.

Hoffman, Jeff, and David Finkel. *Scale: Seven Proven Principles to Grow Your Business and Get Your Life Back*. New York: Portfolio, 2014.

Hoffman, Reid, and Chris Yeh. *Blitzscaling: The Lightning-Fast Path to Building Massively Valuable Companies*. New York: Currency, 2018.

Humble, Jez, Joanne Molesky, and Barry O'Reilly. *Lean Enterprise: How High Performance Organizations Innovate at Scale*. Sebastopol, CA: O'Reilly Media, 2015.

Kawasaki, Guy. *The Art of the Start 2.0: The Time-Tested, Battle-Hardened Guide for Anyone Starting Anything*. New York: Portfolio, 2015.

McGrath, Rita Gunther, and Ian MacMillan. *The Entrepreneurial Mindset: Strategies for Continuously Creating Opportunity in an Age of Uncertainty*. Boston, MA: Harvard Business Review Press, 2000.

Novak, David. *Taking People with You: The Only Way to Make Big Things Happen*. New York: Portfolio, 2013.

Reum, Courtney, and Carter Reum. *Shortcut Your Startup: Speed Up Success with Unconventional Advice from the Trenches*. New York: Gallery, 2018.

Ries, Eric. *The Lean Startup: How Today's Entrepreneurs Use Continuous Innovation to Create Radically Successful Businesses*. New York: Crown Business, 2011.

Savitz, Andrew, and Karl Weber. *Talent, Transformation, and the Triple Bottom Line: How Companies Can Leverage Human Resources to Achieve Sustainable Growth*. San Francisco, CA: Jossey-Bass, 2013.

Sutton, Robert I., and Huggy Rao. *Scaling Up Excellence: Getting to More Without Settling for Less*. New York: Crown Business, 2014.

Wickman, Gino. *Traction: Get a Grip on Your Business*. Dallas, TX: BenBella, 2012.

INDEX

Milton Keynes UK
Ingram Content Group UK Ltd.
UKHW041815300923
429656UK00006B/12/J